Collected Poems

of

Raymond Souster

Volume Three
1962-74

Book design by Michael Macklem

Printed in Canada

PUBLISHED IN CANADA BY OBERON PRESS

This book is for Lia, as always,
for Earle, George and Ron,
and for the memory of William Carlos Williams

THE COLOUR OF THE TIMES (1964) 12
More on Drunken Clocks; Last Beer at the Towne; Eddie Condon at the New Colonial; Ninety Ducks; The Extra Blanket; Easter Sunday; Poem for Francine; Ambulance; Swan, Midhurst Park; The Burial; Blind Girl; Prelude; Loyalist Burial Ground, Saint John; Groundhog's My Nature; Fisherman; Homecoming; Lilac Bush in Winter; Grey Squirrel, Central Park; The Man Who Finds Love on the Subway; Girl in the Blue Bikini; The Problem of Skating; Another Day; The Dogs of Korea; Decision on King Street; Dandelion; To Have the Patience; October Moon; Silence; The Rain is Only the River; This Wind; The Cave; Four Girls at the Corner; The Change; The Fortress; Simile; The Tragedy; The Pink and Blue Balloons; The Wild Wolves of Winter; The Wrapper; The Stone; Beautiful Children; Freeze-Up; They Said; Rainbow Over Lake Simcoe; Black Ant; Air-Force Chaplain; Thrush; Swansea Spring; Spring Waits for Me; Last Ice on Bass Lake; Hawk; The Face of Cleveland; Good Fortune; Ninety in the Shade; Cicada; The Motives; World of the Waterfall; Go Ask; Who Knows; Three Sounds in the Valley; Old Cemetery; The Clock in the Kitchen; Ocean Limited Leaving Bonaventure Station, 1943; In the Barn; Old Man Crossing the Farmyard; Wild Canary; Be the Weed Cutter.

12 NEW POEMS (1964) 61
The Ritual; Flotsam; The Quarrel; Maryrose Visits the Toronto Stock Exchange; Winter Valley; The Roundhouse; Foghorn; The Scream; The Abandon of Cats.

TEN ELEPHANTS ON YONGE STREET (1965) 69
Ten Elephants on Yonge Street; Mechanical Stump-Remover; Wrecking-Ball; Pictures from a Long-Lost World: A Morning in Brussels, 1943; A Death in Rutherford; St. Catherine Street East; The Acorn; Tenement; April Fourth; Mackenzie's House; On Georgian Bay; Pee Wee; The Walk; Some Small

Green Buds; Church Bells, Montreal; "Mr. Hill"; Evergreen in Winter; Great Beast of the Fog; This Lizard of Summer; The Bride; The Whistler; Armadale Avenue Revisited; You are the One Bird Singing; The Unbelievable; Her Highness; Last Bonfire; Metamorphosis; This Last Dopey Fly; Boy Playing with Mud; Bad Luck; Laura Secord; Fireworks; Walking River Ice; Tryst; The Changes; Offering; Twenty-Eight Million Market; Long, Long Winter; Tom Fisher's Mill; All Animals Like Me; Winter Break; The Light; On the Road to Wiarton; Sparrow Supper; Words for Kellie Jones Alone; Wedding Night; Christmas Dinner; My Two Poplars; Nineteenth-Century Music-Box; Gwendolyn MacEwen at the Bohemian Embassy; The Drunk Down the Street; Observation Ward; Sign of the Times; The Parade; Calamity the Cat; Summer Camp for the Blind; Broken Day; Old Farms, Bruce Peninsula; Calling on Leroi; Looking at Old Photographs; The Confidences of Spring; Morning of Grey Rain; Memory of Bathurst Street; Summer Shower; Broken Bottle; King Street Station; Riding Out.

AS IS (1967) 123
The Day Before Christmas; Sunday Morning in the Park; Journey; Into Night; Kensington Market; Kite; Moving Day; Night Over Huron; The Leaf Man; General Brock at Fort George; Jazzman; On the Rouge; The Good Doctor; Funeral Oration; Seven Days of Looking at a Rubber Plant; Night Raider; So Easy to Explain; The White Bedsheet; The Rites; Beyond; At the Airport; Thaw; Can It Be?; Crazy Spring Song; 1944; Maple; The Wall; Twin Sittings; Thickson's; Unadulterated Poetry; Stopping by the Side of the Road; Milk-Chocolate Girl; The House on Indian Road; News of the Day; Nobody's Told the Birds; Montreal '65; Compensation; Air-Raid Practice; A Walk in the Park; Bus Stop; A Picker of Dandelions; *Bocce* Players, September; At the Polanyis'; Boldt's Castle; The Bud; Butterfly on Melinda Street; The Cry; Migra-

tion; The Immigrant; The Farm Out the Sydenham Road; Hurdy-Gurdy in the Snow; The Snows of Summer; The Sirens; Spring Soaking; The Worm; I Like to Imagine; Bill; The Marriage Bit; Never Look Back; The Last Piece of Bread; How Natural is Gas; Weeping Willow, Early Spring; Night with Slow Freights; Red Roses on the Trellis; Funeral Director; Wasp Nest; The Prayer and a Sacrilege; Say Goodbye; John Sutherland, 1919–56; A Christ on Yonge Street; On Our First Day of May; The First Scarlet Tanager.

LOST & FOUND (1968) 197
A Shadow; The Visit; The Interruption; The Bed from Holland; Hallelujah; Pensioners in the Park; For John Pocock's Daughter; Waters; On the Island; The Embarrassment; A Witness from Jehovah; Walking October's Streets; The Roses; Driftwood; The Words; A Sharing; Killing a Bat; Show Time; The Small Coloured Stones; Weeping Willow.

SO FAR SO GOOD (1969) 211
August Garden; How to Skip Stones on a Rough Day; Chasing the Puck; At the Wedding Party; At this Moment; Twelve Daffodils at Easter; The Underpass; Downtown Train; The First Two Acorns; The Song; Walking through Sackville; Good Dog Sam; What the Camera Never Catches; Get the Poem Outdoors; Pomegranates in Studio One; Late Arrival; We were Innocents Then; Backwater; The Chimney; The Angels; Send-Off; Pitching Apples; For Padraig; Battered; The End of February; Garbage in the Morning; Thursday Night Out; Pact; National War Memorial; Cicada Madness; Some Canadians; Shoe-Store; Weeping Willow in Winter; The Dresden Special; Waiting for Rain; Full Blossom; Very Short Poem; The Explanation; The Mirror; Ducks, Five O' Clock, Late November; Ice Valley; The Big Freeze; The Wild One; The Worm from the Centre of the World; The Last Batter.

THE YEARS (1971) 257
There's No Way Out of It; Yeah, Tigers; Old Veterans, Battery
Dinner; The Eye; The Petition; Summer Falling; The Girls of
the Morning; Now We Take You to Biafra; Max; Meeting in
the Subway; Big Al at the Kicking-Horse; Little Boy Lost;
Now the Mulberry's Fruit; La Crosse; A Praying Mantis;
Death on the Construction Site; More Interruptions Like This,
Please; Jewels; Don't Laugh; Top Secret; Grigio; Small House
in a Small Town; A Letter to Biafra; Death Chant for Mr.
Johnson's America; The Hippies at Nathan Phillips Square;
The Confrontation; The Critic; Peace Demonstration; Five
Nighthawks; The Problem; Remembrances; Almost Last Visit
to an Old Town; The Cage; Close to Home; First Snowflake;
The Great White Locusts; Two Taunting Crows; A Kind of
Voyeur; Fool's Day; Mourning Dove; First Report to the
Military Governor; Waiting for the Rain to End; Man With
Clubfoot; The House; Not Really for Publication; It's Not
That Easy; Forecast; Chemnitz Attack, February 14/15, 1945;
Demolition in August; Portrait of the Artist as a Young Man
Well-Rolled in Montreal; For Ikuko From the Two of Us; Old
Lake Light, Hanlan's Point; For Bay Street Charlie.

CHANGE-UP (1974) 323
Yorkville Avenue; In a Moment of Anger; Ottawa for Me;
Tracks in the Snow; Snowplough; The Touch; Shipwrecked;
Pictures from a Long-Lost World: 1912; The End of Summer;
The Sign; First Holiday Morning; February Wind; This Rose;
Holding Hands in the Library; Back Lane; Thirteen Days of
Death; Queen Anne's Lace; Wrecker's Progress; Old Mill by
Floodlight; Now that April's Here; Skater; The Gift; Pictures
from a Long-Lost World: The Stacker, Western Front, 1917;
Last Carry; Bay Street; The Spider Outside Our Window; The
Papers from Hungary; Last Drum-Beat for Rose LaRose.

PREFACE

This is the third volume in a projected four-volume edition of my *Collected Poems 1940–80*. It contains all the poems from the period 1962 to 1974 that I wish to retain in print. Owing to space limitations, however, only the first 28 poems from the collection *Change-Up* (1974) could be included in this volume; the remaining poems will appear in Volume 4. I should note that with one exception all the titles in this book appear in the order in which they were originally published.

The opening collection, *The Colour of the Times* (1964), besides being possibly my best-known book of verse, also marked my first major appearance as a Canadian poet. Its publication was due largely to the encouragement of John Robert Colombo, then trade editor at Ryerson Press, and (although I did not know it at the time) to some stalwart behind-the-scenes campaigning by Ron Everson, then a member of the board at Ryerson. Though described as the "Collected Poems of Raymond Souster," it was in fact a selection of both old and new work, skilfully chosen and edited by John Colombo.

This volume also includes two other of my favourite collections. *As Is*, originally published by Oxford Canada in 1967, was the result of close collaboration with William Toye. Toye, then trade editor at Oxford, worked with me every step of the way, and the end result was, I thought, more than worth every bit of the extra trouble involved. The other title, *So Far So Good* (1969), besides being my initial book with Oberon Press, also gave me the chance to work with Michael Macklem for the first time, another of the few pleasures that have come my way during the long years spent struggling to survive as a poet in Canada.

RAYMOND SOUSTER

The Colour of the Times
(1964)

ſ

MORE ON DRUNKEN CLOCKS

(For Gwendolyn MacEwen)

Our drunken clock has been examined
by the watchmaker down the block,
who says the last time it was cleaned
too much fluid was left in the works,
and that fluid was alcohol.

He has promised to return in a week
a thoroughly sober clock,
which means no more days of work lost
at soul grinding-under jobs,
or appointments missed
with boring, unimportant people;

which brings me around to the wish
that I hope to God somewhere there are still
a few good drunken clocks left
to carry on their same delightful damage.

LAST BEER AT THE TOWNE

We are all a little mad,
my friend,

not just at the edges,
but right down the centre,
deep.

And age does not wither us decently,
it rips up, desolates us,
opens a dark door
onto nothing,
into screaming emptiness:

through which we walk
dead drunk
or chanting poetry,

but still with the living,
my friend.

13

EDDIE CONDON AT THE NEW COLONIAL

"Old Eddie
looks pretty well battered,"
Baldy sitting across from me
tells his pal.

But above all the crash
of glasses, barkeeps' chatter,
the music comes bursting
as unchanged, as honest
as the hard lines of time
laid on your face, Mr. C,

and after fourteen years
not too many things are still as good
or even try to be,
old battered one.

NINETY DUCKS

Charging the dead day
into life with a hoopla
of grunts, cries, quackings,

ninety ducks
like a class of schoolboys,
attack the yellow popcorn
strewn along the bank,
then slide off the slippery ice
one by one into
the cold, dark water,

where they churn and paddle
up, down that narrow passage
hacked out of the ice,
with such abandon, such energy,
that I glow all over
my chilled and miserable
indoor-winter body!

THE EXTRA BLANKET

Somewhere deep in the night
I wake up shivering from cold,

and reaching out,
pull something over me
that is soft and breathes,
has a nose, has lips,
soft hair, folding arms,
hidden crevices and other
warm, wonderful compartments.

O reasons to spare
why winter's never cold
or long enough.

16

EASTER SUNDAY

The day begins
too well. The wind is summer's,
out of season,
the sun, shy behind clouds,
surely will burst through
in brilliance soon.

But rain with thunder
before evening.
Behind the stone rolled away
another and.another
without end.

POEM FOR FRANCINE

From the shining-circus railing of the supermarket's check-out
    counter
(which you use as a swing-bar) to the side street lurking
with the Big Dog, the Stroking Cat, where you try at music
on garbage-cans fallen or upright, where every door holds
a mystery behind it, where house-steps loom
as more than just up or down, where hedges bristle
prickly-soft to your touch, where a flower in the hand
becomes wonderful bouquets: where every day, Francine,
you are pushed one short step further
into our beautiful, terrifying world.

AMBULANCE

Suddenly electrifying
Parkdale's midday quiet,
the siren's hell-calling sound
starts to wail, and we take
the pot-holes, the streetcar tracks
of King Street hurtling west
toward St. Joseph's with a dead-on-arrival
on the stretcher behind us
(my relative, my dead one,
not even this mad noise
can waken you now),

and it can't ever wail
long or loud enough
to atone for your life,
for its waste,
for its years of loneliness,
of misplaced sacrifice,
it can't
and shouldn't even try. . . .

Though as we roar on
toward Sunnyside,
toward the end of this,
I can't somehow feel sad:

you've escaped,
you're free at last,
leaving us behind you
to battle,
to achieve life. . . .

SWAN, MIDHURST PARK

White perfect glide
across what uninspired water!

THE BURIAL

After the censer's last swing
at the church door, hands released
from the casket's handle,

the black hearse leads us
through ten-o'clock summer sunshine
up Keele Street past the thousand deaths
of the slaughter-house animals,
past the new anonymous suburbs
out into open country
timothy-cool, alfalfa-fresh,
with brown barns, browner cows,
and sky a jeweller's blue,
poet's dream.

And feeling so alive
at the cemetery I wanted
to somehow wrench the top
right off your coffin,
girl so young to die,
to have the sun shine down
on your white face to warm it
all the way from here
through the long way over
into eternity.

BLIND GIRL

The blind girl
gropes for the railing, touches it,
and that wood becomes real,
a living force in her hands.

In its place a tree springs up,
with smooth trunk,
branches, leaves
and birds,

which at any moment
may begin to sing!

PRELUDE

Race the water downhill
to the nearest sewer,
let the sun
careen off your winter face
the same way it bounds and rebounds
off the snow left in dirty piles.

But mostly let your mind
strip itself naked,
free of all but music,
sound of water drowning winter
in one crazy flood,

dancing the daftest step
on the black corpse of the snow!

LOYALIST BURIAL GROUND, SAINT JOHN

Three o'clock,
school's out.

Only time of day
the dead really hate,
as the children take
a short-cut through the park,
then sliding over
the flat-lying tombstones
run on and out and away,

taking their warmth, their laughter,
back to the living.

GROUNDHOG'S MY NATURE

Groundhog's my nature:
hole up deep in winter,
walk cautious above ground
in spring and summer,
leave a piece of arm or leg
and a smear of blood
in the crafty hunter's trap
just to hold his interest.

FISHERMAN

Fisherman with an empty basket,
fisherman in a city surrounded
by water no fish can live in,
fisherman still wearing
those thick rubber boots
I've never seen you without,
winter or the hottest summer day.

Crazy old Chinese fisherman,
if I had the money
and the world was a kind place,
I'd fly you home again
to the banks of the Yangtze,
even bribe the fish
to leap into your net,

if the world was a true place,
old fisherman.

HOMECOMING

Good to be back
in the old house. To hear
the toilet's sudden boil and simmer-down,
to walk along the upstairs hall and know
where the floor will creak and not creak,
to find the same cobweb
crouched in that same secret corner,
to feel faithful bed-springs
warm to their work again!

LILAC BUSH IN WINTER

Push your buds, lilac,
much as a young girl
feels her nipples shiver,
then suddenly harden
as her lover fondles her,

as the spring wind tonight
takes you in every branch.

GREY SQUIRREL, CENTRAL PARK

After looking at all those high buildings,
after watching all the people go by,
after having a bellyful of Central Park South
what a pleasure to come back to you!

THE MAN WHO FINDS LOVE ON THE SUBWAY

Some mornings are better than others.

One day you'll find her in the first car,
almost without a word she sits down,
curls up on the seat beside you,
and before the train reaches Queen
you feel you've known her all your life,
and are almost ready for love.

Then there are the black days
when you go from coach to coach
but find she has either escaped you
or accidentally missed your train,
or you even think you see her body
disappearing up the stairs at another stop.

This is madness, you tell yourself,
then start right in dreaming
of how it will be tomorrow.

GIRL IN THE BLUE BIKINI

In broad daylight imagine
the eye of her navel
winked lasciviously at me!

THE PROBLEM OF SKATING

No, Souzy, I don't see
how they do it either—
skimming over the ice
on their wing-tipped blades
with the grace of dancers. . . .

Unless, and this is how
I really think it works—
they're each suspended
on invisible threads
let down from the sky,
lowered slowly until
they almost *seem* to touch the ice. . . .

And of course the children
are so in love with the trick,
and play it so skilfully
that no-one's ever thought
to question it at all—

until you and I, Souzy.

25

ANOTHER DAY

The day opens suddenly, door
into a half-wakened world.

Trains snort,
streetcars loop squealing,
engines gun, reach crescendos,
and this wakes the birds
who in turn wake me:

but still we all wait
through one whole given minute,
for a sign, an excuse,
from anyone or anywhere,
for any reason, good, bad or otherwise,
to pack up the whole useless business once again.

THE DOGS OF KOREA

After your good meal in the mess
here was this young Korean boy
pointing to the dog outside and telling you
he'd bring at least twenty-five
black-market dollars—with you barely making it
to the latrine before you threw up. . . .

But only the next week
passed a poor farmhouse where they were roasting one
on an open spit, and this time you merely shrugged
your shoulders and drove on; you couldn't afford
to lose another meal simply because back home
in Canada a dog could claim more love
than most human beings: here both got none at all.

DECISION ON KING STREET

I watch,
the beggar with the one leg
whose hand holds out pencils, watches

the lady stopped with her back to us,
fumbling in her purse for either
a dime for that pencil or a subway token.

My eyes,
the eyes of this ragged man,
say together:
nothing else in the whole world
at this moment
is of more importance.

DANDELION

Dandelion, if it wasn't
for your impudence
this dull split length of concrete
would never have burst into blossom
even once in its lustreless lifetime.

TO HAVE THE PATIENCE

To have the patience
of waiting to see
how long a rain-drop
hangs to the underside
of the tree branch before it
so swiftly falls.

OCTOBER MOON

The moon up there
on its pass across evening,

a yellow madness
in the eyes.

SILENCE

It's silence that chills us
after the night noises cease
(last radio turned off,
last car's exhaust down the block).

Silence that shouts at us
through the tom-tom
of a clock's ticking,
then reaching up stealthily
to strike us in our beds.

I say "us"
meaning "you"
meaning "me."

THE RAIN IS ONLY THE RIVER

The rain is only the river
grown bored, risking everything
on one big splash.

THIS WIND

This wind comes charging at the house
like a creature unchained, puts its fists
through cracks around windows and gives
curtains enormous breasts, takes a bird
downwind and twists and turns him every way,
bruises tree branches past endurance, leaves them wailing
after each onslaught, then goes careening
over the roof-tops, powdering the air
with snow-sugar.

O but this wind
of December's the same wind we'll later feel
soft as a girl's touch on our face,
warmer even than her embrace,
and coming with the lingering scent
of just-opened lilacs sweeter far than all
but her most mysterious, never-dreamt-of,
long-past-midnight places!

THE CAVE

Deep down in the middle
of this forest a cave
made for me only,
where I often go
to escape from man
and his cruelty,
his desolation.

A small, neat cave
always warm,
always beckoning.

To get there I head
for two far birches,
then slide in through moss
to the waiting
welcome cavern
of her love!

FOUR GIRLS AT THE CORNER

Waiting for a fix
four girls at the corner,
three about eighteen,
the fourth not more
than thirteen, I swear,
not one day more.

All waiting for the Man
to come and take them
for a few short hours
out of misery.

God, the taxi-driver said,

but He hadn't
come along yet either.

THE CHANGE

The river the same,
the ducks, the gulls there
birds I'd seen before,
certainly the lovers
walking with the same arms round,
fingers touching.

Dryness in, stillness from
the long grasses the same
as the leaves were, fallen
on this path a year ago.

But something had changed,
and suddenly it came—
I was really the one
who had been transformed,
who would never walk
by this river the first
warm week of November

quite the same unencumbered
happy fool again.

THE FORTRESS

I will wash the outside
of all the windowpanes,
then bring from the cellar
the storm-windows and fit them
one by one in place.

Having done this
there'll be nothing left to do
but go inside, sit down,
calmly wait for the first snow.

SIMILE

As useless
as the old knife-sharpener
going by and loudly
swinging his bell
on Dominion Day.

THE TRAGEDY

(For Gaston Miron)

After the hearty hand-shake:

"Je ne parle pas anglais."

"Je ne parle pas français."

THE PINK AND BLUE BALLOONS

The pink balloon the colour of her cheeks,
the blue one the colour of her eyes.

Both she holds close to her
as others go pop-pop
at the next table.

If you wish to see anger flare up
from a warm smile, lunge out
with your lighted cigarette.

If you succeed
know that she curses you
under that smile,
once for herself
and once for her baby.

That is, if you dare.

36

THE WILD WOLVES OF WINTER

The wild wolves of winter
swept through these streets last night.

Hate glared in their eyes
like unexploded neon,
wind-whip of their howling a thousand moon-curdling moans,
bared teeth of their hunger endless fields of aching snow.

The wild wolves of winter,
welcome nowhere, clawed at doors and windows,
ripped at roofs, tore at chimney-tops,
kept us wide awake, nervous,
in our warm, sleep-calling beds.
The wind moan. The crazy clawing. The shaken doors.

Then as suddenly were gone,
all was quiet.
We turned a last time in our beds
and slept.

THE WRAPPER

A red-and-yellow
chocolate-bar wrapper
clings to the sidewalk so well
my broom can't dislodge it.

Almost as if
it wants to be thought of
as belonging here.

THE STONE

Rubbed by the centuries,
weed-hidden,
cool to touch
though right under the sun.

How easily you lie there,
how permanent;
useless, yes,
but so necessary!

BEAUTIFUL CHILDREN

Beautiful children
conceived in lust and despair,
beautiful children:

the boy in blue jeans,
the girl too,
age ten and eleven;
the boy slightly ugly,
but if knowing it yet not caring,
the girl beautiful,
and aware of it by the way she tosses
the dark hair down her back,
by the way she walks
in the tight-fitting, shiny jeans—
O she'll be a beauty
in three or four years
who'll have every boy for miles around
tossing sleepless at night wondering how
to get her off into the bush. . . .

Thick-screened though stunted bush beginning
a hundred yards in from the road,
running on into useless swamp,
scattered ponds reflecting empty skies
and leafless trees rotting at their trunks,
that every year seems to inch in closer
to the cleared land lying largely idle,
land slaved over fifty years ago
in desperate hope, now abandoned for what it is,
a bitter joke; land where the rock jags through
at every rise, land never clear of stones,
land worked out, now waiting to be swept back
into bush, into death.

The parents of the beautiful children
young once, now old,
turning to the bottle more and more
as they turn from each other—
he with a pension from shrapnel
in the stomach, fiery lion with booze in him,
sick dog the rest;
she, once girl-beautiful,
now with the care-lines branched across her face,
figure turned shapeless as her life,
brooding often on the four lost children,
beating the two live ones to atone for it. . . .

These beautiful children
conceived in lust and despair,
beautiful children—
going by them on the road
you want to stop, take them with you
to some place, any place else
but this patch of death on the back roads.

But with any luck
they'll make it away themselves,
the boy perhaps joining the army,
the stories of his father ringing in his ears,
where they'll teach him to kill and be a man.
The girl, if she stays that beautiful
and doesn't get pregnant first,
may make Barrie or even Toronto
as a waitress, a factory hand,
may end up respectable and married.

But for now they are only
beautiful children moving through the weeds
of an uprooted pasture toward a sort of barn
hidden behind their tar-papered shack of a home
on a back road nobody uses.

FREEZE-UP

I wonder at what exact moment
(I wish I'd been there)
something or someone said,
"That's the very last drop going over."

And the startled waterfall
suddenly couldn't budge
and knew it was so.

THEY SAID

They said she looked pale
(the birth was a hard one),
they said she shouldn't use shadow
around her eyes anymore.

They said they said they said—
while I was still being shaken
with the miracle of being
in the same room with her again.

42

RAINBOW OVER LAKE SIMCOE

Before the mayor could get to the telephone
to inform his councillors,
so all five could meet
and immediately declare it illegal,

the rainbow had said "Why not?"
and sucked up half of Lake Simcoe,
then after once around the horseshoe
dropped it softly back in Lake Couchiching.

BLACK ANT

Black ant, if I had
but one grain of your energy,
your patience, your devotion,

I would long ago
have become immortal.

43

AIR-FORCE CHAPLAIN

The Pope is in Rome
but the good Father St.-Pierre
(Flight-Lieutenant)
is in Sydney, Cape Breton,

where sharp at eight AM
all dressed up in his best
Sunday-morning blues,
he moves down the rows
of silent airmen's bunks,
to stop at the bed-card
of each faithful one,
where he gives the owner
a sleep-robbing shake.

Then waddles out the door,
leaving in his wake
half a roomful of cursing,
slowly rising boys,
the smoke of crap games
still stinging their eyes,
the poison from blind pigs
still lighting their blood,
the deep sweat of women
still clinging to their skins;

who without breakfast
in half an hour will go
to be cleansed by His Grace,
to be pardoned by Her Love.

THRUSH

A thrush on the farthest-out bough
sings the best song his heart will allow.

And if we haven't liked what we've heard
there's tomorrow and another bird.

SWANSEA SPRING

Down the sliding-swift roller-coaster
of the redwing-blackbird's flight,

then up, over roofs
many tree-tops away,

leaving village, this whole golden world
trembling with spring!

45

SPRING WAITS FOR ME

I don't wait for spring,
spring waits for me.

With a snap of my fingers
I can focus the sun,
with a turn of the head
bring the warm winds on.

So the whole world waits,
eyes me patiently,
for something deep to stir,
to burst inside me,

like the push of a root
or the swoop of a bird!

46

LAST ICE ON BASS LAKE

Tossing the ice in,
crushing it, shredding it
cruelly against the shore.

No knight on any lost battlefield
ever went down with braver armour shining!

The late sun of afternoon knows it
as it walks on diamond-glinting feet
through the heaving death-mass.

Listen—the sound
of a thousand tiny bells tinkling together
in a kind of Angelus,
a fond farewell!

HAWK

Brown shadow of noonday,
sail on a windless sea,
you drift on and over
these last forest trees, then tack, circle round
once, twice, a slight shudder through your wings
keeping you aloft. You see us but give no sign
as you skim across the road,
start the long slow sweep and circle
of the trees again.

Brown shadow of noonday,
as the hour builds to its frenzy
of heat, of crickets' cries,
only you are calm above it all,
cold and omnipotent as fate.

THE FACE OF CLEVELAND

The face of Cleveland looks out at me
at four in the afternoon
from a bar on Euclid Avenue.

Black face with eyes that don't see me,
with eyes that look past everything
then come back empty,
come back overflowing with darkness.

Green lawns of Shaker Heights,
stone grace of the Museum,
I have left my eyes on a barstool on Euclid Avenue,
I can't see the blooms on the dogwood faced with all this
    darkness.

GOOD FORTUNE

She waits patiently
for fortune to come to her,
like a steeplechase winner,
like the million to the missing heir.

She goes to see the priest,
reads her catechisms over,
then waits for the miracle
to finally happen.

And I'd tell her
(only she wouldn't believe me)
life isn't a matter of luck,
of good fortune,

it's whether the heart can keep singing
when there's really no reason
why it should sing at all.

Yes, I'd tell her,
only she'd start in crying,
her with a heart that never had
the excuse for a single song.

NINETY IN THE SHADE

So hot by the afternoon
a rock on the cooler side
of the garden tilted slightly,
and three fat sleepy slugs
invited me under.

CICADA

Cicada,
our nerves trigger-taut from the heat
fight for balance on the crazy high-wire
of your screech.

THE MOTIVES

The dog barks at me,
I bark right back at him,

one inventing an enemy,
one despairing of a friend.

WORLD OF THE WATERFALL

We enter the world
of the waterfall:

world that climbs
with the uprush of two
stretch-necked ducks
from the river's dream
to the towering cliffs
of the valley defended
by an oak stockade
tiered with living green
to the start of the sky.

Our voices sound unreal,
far away. Only our eyes
do not betray us.

If we could sleep
we would sleep,
if we could dream
we would dream;

but the valley holds us
to a sound of water,
only if its stops
will we breathe,
will we move again,

only if it stops
or gives us a sign
will we return
to that other world.

GO ASK

Grey squirrel, go ask
the sumachs on the slope
why they bleed so.

WHO KNOWS

Who knows, my heart
may beat again
quick as the slap
of the first skipping-rope
of spring.

54

THREE SOUNDS IN THE VALLEY

Three sounds in the valley
spoke and stayed in my ear—
low babble of the river
in the open ice channels,
echoed crack of an axe
against a stubborn tree
on the height above.

And to stir my mood
the roused, simple chirp of a bird
too shy to show himself,
yet unwilling that his song
should remain unheard.

OLD CEMETERY

(Queen's, New York)

Last night, chasing after
a red-ball moon through Queen's
on the way to the airport,

we passed a cemetery
hemmed in between
the throughway and the gasworks,
as though even death
was being crowded out,
as though the dead
had no place left to lie
in simple dignity.

Each skinny tombstone
seemed a hand upraised
to warn us of something
perhaps just beyond
the next curve in the road,
or in the tunnel's
reverberating pit,

a hand of warning
left behind in an instant,
a benediction.

THE CLOCK IN THE KITCHEN

Though clearly the clock
in the kitchen had died
at 6.41 this cold morning,
and time, so to speak, was dead,

I still found myself shaving
the same lifeless face,
dressing up once more
the same roly-poly body,
munching on the same breakfast food,
then hurrying the same two blocks
to catch the same streetcar
that I had the day before.

Though very plainly the clock
(or time) had stopped,
I sat watching the same
deadly streets blur by,

with only the thinnest of hopes
that the next morning time chose to die
all this world would somehow die too.

OCEAN LIMITED LEAVING BONAVENTURE STATION, 1943

... Montreal somewhere back there
alive and breathing in the darkness.
City to take along in sleep tonight,
to walk down its streets
arm-in-arm again
with a hundred poets!

IN THE BARN

If we both lie quiet,
if we make no sound
louder than your warm breath
now close on my neck,

perhaps the others
won't find us hidden here
in the granary bin,

perhaps they'll even go away,
leaving us grain-covered, breathing dust,
the trickling sweat on our bodies
now one rivulet of joy.

OLD MAN CROSSING THE FARMYARD

Chickens scratching the dust stop their squabbling as if on a
    signal,
a cat wakes up, would dearly like to stretch himself,
but remains instead motionless, not a whisker quivering,
a bird lights on a fence-post, sees the cat,
knows it can mean his life, but his wings somehow stay at
    rest—

for the old man has emerged from the back door, and shuffling
    half a step at a time
(as if on the edge of the world and not wanting to go hurtling
    off),
inches toward the barn, the years pushing at his back,
squeezing both his legs, pressing in at his throat,
with whatever still lives in him whispering above his frantic
    heart-beat
"Go on, go on!"

59

WILD CANARY

Blow the wind as it may
through the tall meadow-grass,
you ride on your weed-stalk
with the ease, the poise
of a high-wire artist
who takes every bend,
every perilous swaying
so indifferently,
all the time pecking hard
at the ripe fruit before you,
intent on getting your fill.

Then O how the wind must tire
of your indolence,
for with one great gust
he flings you from your perch,
up and over in a sudden
yellow flash that blinds
almost like the midday sun.

BE THE WEED-CUTTER

Be the weed-cutter
steaming slowly through the lagoons,
working quietly and well,
your blades searching out
a clearer, deeper channel
than has been before.

12 New Poems
(1964)

THE RITUAL

One altar-boy picking his nose,
another yawning,
all through the tedium of the Mass.

FLOTSAM

With the tide out,
with the last inch of water gone,
with only salt smell, green phlegm
of seaweed rubbing the piers—

down there, right at the bottom
of the muck, among the pile-up
of wood chunks, bottles,
all the strange garbage of the sea,

look, the corpse
(eyes still shining)
of our long-drowned youth!

THE QUARREL

No wonder I can't sleep
on this downstairs sofa,
it's really only made
for her curled cat's body,

that now, in the middle of the night,
tosses troubled
(or so I like to think)
on our upstairs bed,

while my body,
even more troubled,
tosses here.

63

MARYROSE VISITS THE TORONTO STOCK EXCHANGE

If the shouting bothers you
cover your ears, my lady,
if the disorder jars you
reflect that in this disorder
lies the strictest order.

Then, when you finally
can't stand any more
of this interplay of commerce,
why, simply move down
to the middle of the trading,
shake your hips a couple
of wonderful times and bring
this whole damn farce
to a paper-strewn halt.

WINTER VALLEY

Straight up the valley's
frozen afternoon,
as one with my feet
fighting snow,
hearing trees moan
as they crouch
in wind-fear.

Now with the sun gone
and cold pressing cold
on an iron world,
I feel to my bones
that dumb dark,
that aching loneliness—
North's
and none other.

Then hurry on,
sensing death close behind,
stalking his own.

65

THE ROUNDHOUSE

That first real year
I pitched baseball
we played straight across
from the roundhouse on St. Clair,

and every time
I got jammed up good
in a three-and-two count,
I'd simply stall a little
till a black screen of smoke
blew across from its chimney,
then wind up and throw one
right down the gut
with no worries at all. . . .

But like everything else
that was too good to last—
the next year they tore down
my handy old roundhouse,
and I only finished seven
of my fifteen starts,

all the smoke gone forever
you might say
from my fast one.

FOGHORN

The foghorn lulls you to sleep
but keeps me only restless and awake:
you, two minutes' walk away
from that lighthouse at the long pier's end,
where the horn moans through on the minute
its four short lamentations:

with me far from your island,
across harbour, across city,
far, far from your door
where the foghorn rocks you in its arms

but gives me only nightmares
of sinking ships, good people screaming
as they drown in darkness,

while the spider fog
stifles all cries and draws
its tight net tighter over all.

THE SCREAM

The scream hurled
hits the wall, slips down
garden-flower wallpaper
to the floor, then gathering speed
like a trapped bat,
flaps up my legs,
clawing all my body,
bites arms,
stabs at finger-tips.

Then goes, finally over,
leaving silence
never heavier,
deadlier.

THE ABANDON OF CATS

The abandon of cats
making love in the snow,

enough to send shivers
through our warm, lazy bed!

68

Ten Elephants on Yonge Street
(1965)

TEN ELEPHANTS ON YONGE STREET

Just about everything,
everyone
has passed up or down—

William Lyon Mackenzie's boys
on the quick way down
from Montgomery's Tavern,
Year of Tyrants, 1837.

Wendell Wilkie smiling
his 1940 smile,
with planes overhead
and the crowds gone wild,
the year he could have made
Prime Minister!

But until today
never elephants:
ten grey eminences moving
with the daintiest of steps
and the greatest unconcern
up the shadowy canyon.

Too bored to yawn
or toss the fools riding them,
they slowly twist their trunks
while emptying their bowels
at a pace that keeps
the two men following
with shovels and hand-cart
swearingly busy.

MECHANICAL STUMP-REMOVER

Evil-whirling teeth
chew the tree-stump
with crazy appetite.

Even a woman
would be hard pressed to cut
deeper wounds with her tongue.

71

WRECKING-BALL

The wrecking-ball
of Greenspan
of Teperman
reverberates on King Street,
twisting steel,
smashing brick and stone
to a levelled-out stretch of waste
on which the sun
uneasily shivers.

Battering-rams
O unholy pendulums
of time
of change
of inner restlessness.

As if man,
the bored child toying with his blocks,
must as the whim
takes his hands be able
in a moment's flash
to sweep his playthings
ingloriously down.

PICTURES FROM A LONG-LOST WORLD:
A MORNING IN BRUSSELS, 1943

Granted the most subtle torture that in which the victim knows each step of his pain but is powerless to change it in any way—

Then become this moment the young French-Canadian airman of twenty, who, having watched in the cellar of the Rue Royale the most expert monsters of the Gestapo stalk round on cat-silent shoes behind the line of prisoners (their faces each held six inches back from dripping walls), lashing out with thick rubber truncheons now at this head, now at that, quite at random, totally at whim, never the same pattern quite repeated.

Knowing this to stand in line yourself, lips held tightly together until the first searing terror of your face smashed against the stone without any warning, pain in your bleeding nose like a knife-slit, lips moving tremblingly now in silent prayer, Holy Mary, Mother of God, as you wait for the sound of footsteps which never comes, as you wait for an end, any end. . . .

A DEATH IN RUTHERFORD

(In memoriam W.C.W.)

We can't argue the right
of your body to be lowered
into peace:
> but nothing else
can be allowed to rot,
mix with dust.

You belong
to so many of us.

74

ST. CATHERINE STREET EAST

(For Louis Dudek)

Beer on a hot afternoon?
What else in this Bon Marché of the World,
earth's narrowest, most crowded rabbit-run,
sweating under loud sunshine that glints off
baby-carriages, tin cups of beggars, silver balls of pawn-shops,
making the rouge-layered, powder-dipped girls
squint hard, but not taking anything away
from that free-swinging walk on their stilt-heels. . . .

Beer you said? Well, it's right back here
behind giant cheeses, thick wienerwurst truncheons,
hungry smells of bread, nose-prickling perfumes of coffee.
Look, the cold-sweated bottles count up
to an even dozen, and we fight our way
past the check-out girl to the street
where sun glintings, traffic noise, heat-breath
hit us, then stun us. Every face in every window
of these buildings watching as we go
down the steaming pavement, on and out of this jungle
where the dead are never buried by the living,
but crowd onto buses, sit late at bar-stools,
or wait in the darkness of always-airless rooms.

THE ACORN

Our world an acorn
in the teeth of a squirrel.

We wait and we wait
for him to nibble through.

TENEMENT

Jammed to the street's edge, plagued with traffic whine,
the old house doesn't seem to care
how fast paint chips off, whether shingles hold,
if only it can die.

But the Japanese children crowding the verandah
like a perfect set of pins to my bowler's eye,
are so alive in their hand-me-down clothing
that I wouldn't count on this house dying easily,
say, any more than George Brown's farther down the block.

Just covering up its ears
against the cries of twenty lungs re-echoing through
three pulsing floors should keep it much too busy
to ever think of death again!

76

APRIL FOURTH

I jumped in our bed
as suddenly the snow
felt itself slipping,
clawed wildly once or twice,
then slid with slow thunder
off the roof.

77

MACKENZIE'S HOUSE

(William Lyon Mackenzie, 1795–1861: for Herb Whiteley)

Bond Street at noon-hour:
kids in the St. Michael's schoolyard
break the mood the cathedral
starts pushing up toward heaven. . . .

But their cries snuffed out, completely silenced
with the slam of this front door,
with one turn of its giant key,
and we've moved a century back
into Grandmother's Toronto. . . .

Believe a young woman played this piano,
that another kept pace on the recorder,
that dinner was served to company here
in the stiff-chaired room,
that up these stairs the man himself
climbed to his prisoner's study,
sat at his desk
unable to write the words
that his lips and mind formed
(man once worth a thousand pounds
of His Majesty's blood money,
man hounded by creditors,
man once carried on the crowd's shoulders
by torchlight, now the broken one
slumped in his chair. . . .)

But the house breathes no defeat,
builds a quietness through the rooms, a serenity,
except in the parlour where a glint
of sunlight catching his portrait
throws back fire from the eyes,
accents the fighter's chin.
                              "A singularly
wild-looking little man with red hair,
waspish and fractious in manner,
one of that kind of people
who'd not sit down content
under government of an angel. . . ."

The door slams hard behind us,
the key scraped in the lock sends us back
to Bond Street once more,
the noise, the hurry, the emptiness
of an all-inglorious present. . . .

While inside the caretaker
climbs the echoing stairs
to his third-floor garret,
and as on a signal
the ghosts come alive again. . . .

79

ON GEORGIAN BAY

Ridge on this rock-ledge gouged out
by the last ice-glaciers,
rock under my feet
fired by ages of sun,
rubbed by centuries of wave-smash.

Rock under my feet,
blue water to the meeting of sky,
sun, wind lifting as a kiss.

Stand proudly as Champlain
must have stood, head dizzy
with distances, only seeing
new glory for France and his King;
or like that first Huron
down on his knees, summoning up
with all heart and soul prayers
to the great and jealous
gods of this place.

PEE WEE

(For A. J. M. Smith)

When you approach the gates,
Pee Wee,
blow just one whisky note
and even St. Peter
will know who he's letting in.

THE WALK

Cane feeling the way,
the old Indian woman
inches out her door,
and makes it regardless
through the weeds surrounding
her shack on the crouched side
of a hill as you leave
Blind River behind.

SOME SMALL GREEN BUDS

Some small green buds
urged on by the rain,
grown passionate with sun,

may give us lilacs tomorrow—
and the spring!

CHURCH BELLS, MONTREAL

Against the hard clear
ring of the bells

measure that quick whispered
tick of our lives.

"MR. HILL"

"Mr. Hill" my mother calls it
(though it doesn't really need
another name, as being a plant
it must already have one).

Named for a friend of her family
who brought it to her garden
one spring night in 1919,
and that very weekend
was drowned in a canoe up North.

Kept by my mother all these years
and tended with the greatest love.
Then, to preserve the legacy,
one part of it was planted last year
in this garden, where it fights
its running battle with cutworms,
green tattered leaves
spread in summer toward the sun.

Fights so well, though, my darling,
it's not hard to believe
it may outlive us all.

EVERGREEN IN WINTER

What else may save us,
what else give us hope?

Small evergreen bush,
hold your head high
above the mounting
wasteland of the snow.

GREAT BEAST OF THE FOG

All that's evil
hunches outside my window,
all that's foul
crouches beside my door.

Great beast of the fog,
for three days and nights
I've endured the smell of you,
the taste of you bitter,
gone stale in the mouth.

Great beast of the fog,
grow tired of our curses,
our bored, lifeless faces;
go, leave us all tomorrow,
your last shadow piercing
those floodgates to the sun.

THIS LIZARD OF SUMMER

Heat forked in its tongue
this lizard of summer
licks almost lovingly
each inch of our bodies.

THE BRIDE

In the late light of afternoon
you stood, wedding-gown
dizzy virginal swirl
of white all about you,
while I waited speechless
for your hand to wave,
your eyes give me some slight sign.

Now early this morning
stand naked, gown fallen
wildly about your feet,
no shame at all on your face as you turn
that bugle flesh for all to see.

While the young window-dresser fusses
with the new bridal dress of the day
to fit about your mannequin shoulders.

85

THE WHISTLER

Yesterday you laughed and said
my whistling would wake the dead.

Today all the whistling I could do
would never, never waken you.

86

ARMADALE AVENUE REVISITED

Street of my boyhood
(I lived right around the corner),
quiet, leaf-heavy street
of West Toronto.

Here, behind that house, in that lane,
from garage roofs we ambushed
the Nelles Avenue gang,
pinned them down first with catapults,
then, out of acorns,
forgot all our strategy
and ran like hell.

Out this door on Christmas Day
of all days, that queer girl came walking,
nightgown and all,
and even the snow underfoot
didn't seem to waken her.

At this number lived
the two grease-monkey boys
(their Stutz Touring shined
to a blinding dazzle),
who the odd time took me
as heart-pounding passenger
out the wide Queen Elizabeth Way,
to run her up, then gun her
past eighty on a straight stretch,
with the added spice
of perhaps a speed-cop
showing up out of nowhere.

On this front lawn
I pounded and bloodied
my next-to-worst enemy,
and curiously found
it wasn't fun anymore. . . .

But tonight it's only ghosts
I see around these houses,
all the old gang gone,
every one of them;
some killed in our war,
some from natural causes,
the rest, I can safely guess,
growing fat, middle-aged
much like me.

But not one of them
comes back here, I'm sure,
they've got better sense—

just the crazy poet
still well hooked on the past,
and a sucker for memories.

YOU ARE THE ONE BIRD SINGING

You are the one bird singing
in a dead tree toward nightfall.

I am the one lonely man
standing in the wings of the evening,

listening to impeccable arias
rise from your prima-donna throat.

THE UNBELIEVABLE

Hidden somewhere behind
this flower shop or whatever
fronted King Street there,

two trees or skeletons of trees,
still growing, still fighting to stay alive
in a place where no life was meant to be.

And, just think, not one of us
knew this until today,
when, with buildings levelled,
we looked across this brick-and-rubble wasteland
and saw the unbelievable—

these scrawny limbs, poor arms,
straining upward to reach the sun.

HER HIGHNESS

Yellow-green-eyed cat,
now you've grown tired
of Cleopatra's barge,
you come queening it
across our back lawn,
curious to see what sacrifice
human or otherwise
we'll be able to manage.

LAST BONFIRE

Up the flue of the sky
go my forty years
leaf after smoking leaf.

90

METAMORPHOSIS

Now the leaves are fallen,
now the green-veined beauties
are all dead, lying there
in crisp, splintered piles,

they are only something
in the way, a nuisance,
and I rake them up,
cursing when they wheel away
on the skate of a wind.

Then rest at last, out of breath,
looking down at the brimming baskets,

my beautiful leaves, my green-veined beauties,
now garbage like everything else.

91

THIS LAST DOPEY FLY

This last dopey fly of November,
not enough strength in his wings
to push him a yard through the air,
or enough in his legs to walk him
far enough away from me,

waits patiently to be put out of misery,
and when he finds I'll not oblige,
shrugs whatever he uses for shoulders,
then starts in again to stay alive
by clinging to this window-glass,
where he prays he'll find a little warmth
left behind by that arch-betrayer,
old sluggard, morning sun.

BOY PLAYING WITH MUD

No baker ever kneaded more lovingly
bread-roll or loaf than this boy
in the early sun mixing his mud-ball
back and forth, one hand to the other,

not worrying what he can make of it,
the feeling of roundness, of wetness,
of sand in his palms and on his fingers
enough for him and his child's mood,
and me and this whole
lazy summer morning.

BAD LUCK

This week my luck was all bad;
met her not once but twice
on Victoria Street up from King,
the other time Queen near Church.

I should stay away from those streets,
but one must have somewhere to go;
you can't keep walking around
the same block day after day
just because you don't want to meet
the heavy woman with the limp,
the woman with the crazy look,
old winter hat pulled over her face—

the woman who walks carrying all her belongings,
talking mostly to herself, except when she curses
someone who passes by
and above all this city
that bore her and will watch her die
with the same beautiful indifference
you'd show yourself
to a cat tearing at a mouse.

LAURA SECORD

Lady, long part of our history,
would you perhaps have been so eager
that time to drive those silly cows
before you through the forest mile on mile,
risking who-knows-what indignities
at the hands of the invaders,

had you known you would end up
the name on the box for a brand
of over-sweet chocolates?

94

FIREWORKS

Who knows what mysterious forces,
erupting powers lie
in the secret heart
of these fireworks?
The next Roman candle
may well torch a city,
the next cannon-cracker
crash a whole block down.

No wonder the child
bends over so gingerly
with his lighted match—
no wonder he jumps back,
trembling with joy,
as the sputtering fuse
snakes headlong down
to that last moment, which
may destroy us all!

WALKING RIVER-ICE

There must be at least
six good inches of ice
between me and the gurgle
of unseen water.

Still, I walk with care,
a small nagging fear
hard behind on my heels.

It's no secret, the river
would dearly like me
under not over
that good six inches
of its frozen, undefeated pride.

TRYST

The night rain over them,
his raincoat under.
Her sobs—to smother them
that crash of thunder!

96

THE CHANGES

I can remember when you
were a man we all feared, shaken up
at the sound of your voice, often tortured
by the crazed look in your eyes,
raked over time and again
by your broadsides, your salvoes of fury.

Then meeting today years later
the withered, beaten shell of that man,
I understand you more, sensing most
of your bitterness drained away at last,
leaving you even human again, one of us.

And it does me no good, even pains
to see death's yellow shadowing your face.

◦

OFFERING

In your eyes
my own life heaves,
breaks, even smashes,

in your eyes
suddenly without love.

TWENTY-EIGHT MILLION MARKET

Looking down on the Pit
as Norris called it,
or the floor (as these know it)
of the Stock Exchange:

looking down
at lime or orange coats, shouting faces,
carnations in the buttonholes wading through
white scum of paper to the trading-posts:

standing here with my mouth wide open
in the visitors' gallery, one more of a crowd
with obviously nothing better to do
in their hard-earned lunch-hour,

I watch the illuminated tickers spew up
another vomit of prices and symbols,
wondering what exact quote will slip mink
around the shoulders of what carefully sheltered mistress,
what plunge of the crazy seesaw will force
a hand to an overdose or more crudely towels
stuffed tightly under the door and around the windows....

Amazed that anything else can exist in our buy-and-sell world,
I stare from this balcony with bedlam pounding my ears,
waiting for something to crack, to explode,
to go finally mad.

LONG, LONG WINTER

From the sun today some warmth,
with enough glare to keep the eyes
dancing spectrums for hours.

For which be very thankful.
Anything more asked in March
may be refused in April
or even May.

Besides, confess—
you have almost begun to enjoy
this death-in-life.

TOM FISHER'S MILL

Tom Fisher,
wherever you got the stone from,
whatever mortar you used
to build this mill of yours
(sturdy-upright still
through flood and fire
for a century or more),

I would like to own some,
perhaps shape them into poems;

for the mill has seen you
into the grave, and with luck
will be around to shed
no tears on mine.

ALL ANIMALS LIKE ME

All animals like me
now get themselves out of the cold
and into some kind of lair
cavernous or small,

to curl up more like a ball
than anything else and sleep
an untroubled sleep of snow,

which sifting down endlessly white
and curdled thick as cream
makes the four-poster of a dream.

WINTER BREAK

Enough chill in the air
to remind that winter
could strike back again.

But the snow-piles run
leaking onto the pavements,
gutters carrying down
the drip to the sewers—
that sound the good sound
of falling water.

Nothing else in the darkness
but the rheumy eyes
of houses looking out,
to discover a man
head down whom the vast night
quickly swallows.

THE LIGHT

Walking out one evening
past abandoned houses
where the subway will run some year,

a downstairs light
flicked on in one,
cut flame for a breath,
then snapped back to darkness.

Lovers, I thought, and very young.
Who else would stand the January chill
to take love on the cold boards
of that place?

And walking on, wished them well,
wished them too all the heat their bodies
could rub together, melt together,
in that hard-breathing dark.

ON THE ROAD TO WIARTON

don't want to disturb her—
she's so intent on taking
her swing all the long way up
to the sky—that I hate to call out—

but I'm lost and need help from someone,
so I yell and she runs right over:
blue eyes, platinum hair
point back the way I've come,

while her voice says for certain that it's still
the one road in the world for her.

SPARROW SUPPER

Intent on their supper
which they eat with relish
among the thick grasses;

yet, never straying
beyond that borderline
where no more than the flick
of a finger sends them up,

nervous scattering of leaves
tossed about a mother-watching sky.

WORDS FOR KELLIE JONES ALONE

Kellie, watch close over Mice,
he's a very small cat and so young,
while they tell me a Thirteenth Street rat
is the meanest there is
and the biggest thing in the world
next to Texas.

WEDDING NIGHT

What more can I say
about the stupidity of hotels
after the mix-up of the beds. . . ?

Add to it now
a fuse blown somewhere,
with all lights out the last
eternity of an hour,
while reaching up from the street
a dozen floors below
the sirens of fire-engines
chilling, re-chilling
the summer dark.

You hold yourself tight against me.
Tears come and your body shakes
from I suppose partly fear, partly joy—
whatever draws two opposites
together more than apart.

Easily, beloved,
this will be the longest night
of our lives. . . .

CHRISTMAS DINNER

The dinner fine—
my mother and father
not looking one day older,
my wife busily eating
her net weight in turkey,
my mother-in-law
a miniature *donna*.

But spoiling it all
(at least for me)
the sad brown eyes
of the student from India,
who sits alone
at a table in the corner
of the busy dining-room.

MY TWO POPLARS

Now two jagged stumps
in a stink of resin
around which flies swarm.

And tomorrow even
these last markers gone
of dawn-birds' clamour,
of leaves' shake-shimmer,

where all four seasons
had birth, flowered, died,
where earth touched heaven.

Two giants of the earth
have been struck down here,
leaving us the poorer,
diminished forever.

NINETEENTH-CENTURY MUSIC-BOX

Shining silver strikers
(one moment angry wasps,
the next placid butterflies),

still make the music
of lost memories
within that fully wound
repetitive music-box

the past is.

GWENDOLYN MACEWEN AT THE BOHEMIAN EMBASSY

It's sinking our ship,
water pouring in
overhead and all around—

we're sinking and yet
you stand calmly there
reading poems of Jerusalem,
of Cyrus the Persian
and the giant bow that broke,
while the water sucks over us
with a greedy, drinking sound.

You say you'll never write
another love-poem,
and I know we're all doomed
as I listen for the water
that will reach up and choke
every word in your throat.

THE DRUNK DOWN THE STREET

Almost every night
the drunk down the street
swears at his wife, then curses
the neighbourhood
and every person in it,
but that dog of his—never.

Even a drunk
knows when he's got it made—
someone to sit at his feet
who never complains or talks back,
same tomorrow as today.

Even a drunk knows
when he's down to his very last friend.

OBSERVATION WARD

"An old fellow
cut both his wrists last night,"
he tells me, then adds
to see what my face shows—

"this morning
I looked the longest time
at a razor-blade."

SIGN OF THE TIMES

This man who carries so slowly
the sandwich-board up Yonge Street

to which is attached an obscene
swollen hot-dog, together with
a floating-out-in-space
moon saucer of a hamburger

looks (damn you all)
really hungry.

THE PARADE

I can't thrill anymore
to the drum-rolls, the loud brass
of bands on parade.

I remember too many faces
that marched off behind them
to distant, anonymous death,
betrayed by the heat and blare
of these Devil's instruments,

which chill my bones now.

CALAMITY THE CAT

Calamity the Cat
curled up in our flowerbed.

Late afternoon. Though nothing stirs
but breathing's rise and fall,
her nerves stay trigger-ready,
bent-spring alert,
                can rouse her
with a wrong foot's move,
a threatening gesture, to claw's ready,
lightning's pounce,
                  straight at our foolish
undefended throats.

SUMMER CAMP FOR THE BLIND

Tell me, blind man,
why it had to be today of all days
that I had to meet you, stare into the mirror
of your face, feel the darkness
in my own soul streaming
through the slits in your eyes?

While around me the beach sand
outshone the sun, the water of the lake
lay smooth as breasts in my hands,
and the breeze rousing pine-tops
blew these words through my head

BEGIN TO LIVE

BROKEN DAY

I don't care
how high the clouds are,
how white they curdle
in the whey of the sky,
or if the sun
is kind to the flowers,
or why the wind
plays at storms in the trees:

the robin hiding
in the garden bushes
has a broken wing.

112

OLD FARMS, BRUCE PENINSULA

Death must come hard
to these old farms waiting
for the weeds to cover them.
Houses rot in the sun
till doors slip their hinges,
windows sag and hole up
their shame with much spider-smoke,
barns rot in the rain,
roofs bare-plucked skeletons,
with weathervane winds
always in on the kill.

But these farms wait with dignity
for the thistle to climb,
the goldenrod thicken,
for that final falling,
that touch-to with earth,
then sleep with only
some warm stars above.

113

CALLING ON LEROI

That night as the taxi left us
in front of Number 324,
no faces were looking out
from the high, narrow windows,
CUBA, SI. YANQUI, NO
had been blotted out
from the sign below them.

Only the garbage-cans
beside the mysterious door,
only the candles still alight
in that magical street window,
though the Professor was gone—
Profesora Luz, Palmista,
our Reader and Adviser,
had yielded to the police
and gone the way of all light,

and Thirteenth Street
looked like any other street
only dustier, dirtier,
with only the children,
the beautiful, white-faced children
on the curb and at doorways,
alive in the devil's heat.

LOOKING AT OLD PHOTOGRAPHS

(Columbus Grads Baseball Club, 1940)

Vitore, Bugala, Moszyniski, where are you now,
Angelis, Croswell, Calgone, what has time done with you?

You wouldn't remember me—the kid brought up
from the juniors for a taste of senior ball—
but I remember so well all of you
after twenty years and more, just like yesterday. . . .

Was it down at Belleville I had my first under-age beer,
sitting proudly in the men's room with the rest of you,
glass in front of me, and liking the taste of it
so I didn't have to pretend?
Was it up at Eglinton Park with Rose Jewellers
that they called us "dirty Wops" and baseball bats went
      swinging
at more than just fastballs?
What night did we walk in our spikes
all the way from Stanley Park to Christie Pits
by the back lanes?

That was our last year of baseball: the War waited for us.
No more dusty hours on the diamond, hand-throbbing sting
      of the bat
stroking line-drives, no more third strikes
with a roundhouse curve. . . .

The War waited for us, to take us, to grind us,
at the end of that season!

O Krycia, Wagman, McDowell, heroes of my youth,
where are you now? And where am I?

THE CONFIDENCES OF SPRING

On the first warm day
(walk on the east side of Yonge Street
to get the toasting goodness of the sun),

face of the old man beautiful
as he tells me the manner
of his wife's sudden dying in his arms.

Against this the words
of the young poet almost right after him,
words unworthy of winter-melting sunshine,
almost shameful beside the face
of that old man turned to the world
with nothing in his briefcase but memories.

But on such a day
what does one expect
from an old man but hope,
from a young man but tiredness—

what else makes this hour
shine so and almost sing?

MORNING OF GREY RAIN

Morning of grey rain
bringing alive the grasses,
pushing the worms up
for three happy robins
who, beak down, work hard
against time and weather,

knowing well as I
that nothing waits,
that nothing stays,
that only the ultimate
emptiness of earth
is really certain,

that weeks may not bring us
such a minor blessing
as another exquisite
morning of grey rain.

MEMORY OF BATHURST STREET

"Where are you, boy?"
my Aunt Maggie's calling,
but I can't hear her
in my attic eyrie,
where I watch the heat
swirl up from the tar roofs,
waiting for the cry
of the bearded rag-picker
down the lane from Ulster Street.

"Where are you, boy?"
my Uncle Jim's calling,
but I can't hear him
for the cooing of birds
inside this pigeon-coop
at the back of the garden,
where I scrape up the droppings
to earn my allowance.

"Where are you, boy?"
my Aunt Lizzie's calling,
but I can't hear her
from the upstairs sitting-room,
as I turn the pages
of my favourite book
where the Highlanders lie
in the blood of their death
on green Spion Kop.

SUMMER SHOWER

Hunched together at the bus-stop
north of Serpent River,

three Indian girls,
being soaked to the skin
from the downpour, stare hard

as our cars flash by,
not with envy
or with anger, certainly,

but more resignation,
that in this world
every time it rains
some people will come out
wet and some dry

with no-one in between.

BROKEN BOTTLE

As it was before—
utilitarian at best,
really nothing—

now lying smashed
in small jagged pieces
on the cellar floor,

it takes on shapes,
strange colours,

which could never happen
quite the same way again,
anytime,
anywhere,

this suddenly-become-
unique beer bottle.

KING STREET STATION

The train
braking in

its wheels underneath
tonight almost beckoning.

RIDING OUT

Wide awake as morning
I lie in bed counting
the last minutes out
before rising to drive
through sleep-dripping streets
to the station at the other end of town.

Where at three I'll ride out
in the front diesel cab
of the Transcontinental,
hand ready on the horn
as we make the first crossing
and head on north and west.

Through the night we'll salute
nodding towns, lonely villages,
each whistle-blast moving out
across hills to sink down
into valleys where mists lie chilling,
then re-echo, reverberating back
to my head, through my body.

Headlights soaking up
the mystery ahead, my restless giant
thunders on toward dawn or oblivion.

As Is
(1967)

THE DAY BEFORE CHRISTMAS

(For David Donnell)

My best Christmases
are all behind me. Grandmother lifting
the done-to-perfection bird
grease-dripping from the pan,

my brother and I Christmas morning
out of bed at six-thirty.
I suppose the house shivered to the sudden sharp
tearing of gift-wrap by excited fingers.

This Christmas Eve mid-afternoon
too many years later, I wander downtown,
feeling if possible worse
than most drunks set adrift from their office parties.

Birks' windows bulge and glow
with the totally conspicuous.
There's something fairy-queer about coloured lights
hung above the stink of bus exhausts.

Every store hums, an angry honey-hive,
as if wartime and rationing were back.
I picture patient clerks behind counters
walking on what they can't believe are feet.

Skaters on the fancy rink at City Hall
seem impatient of old waltzes. They dart,
sudden bright goldfish flashing below Revell's
scooped clam-shells blinking underwater eyes.

My heart's with the skaters, though my mood
is more with Adam Beck, bronzed sober head
splitting the traffic of the Avenue,
where on that republic's black consul door I see

or seem to see a holly wreath hung, through which
napalm-skinned faces, dying eyes stare out
at me, this city, and core-rotted world,
to riddle us with bleeding, gaping questions.

1966

125

SUNDAY MORNING IN THE PARK

You are being observed
by water half-crawling
under crystal-clear ice.
It looks up at you
standing on the wooden bridge,
sees your much-too-sober
winter-morning face,
almost feels your limbs
shivering in the early cold,
and wonders if you'll be there
when the ice strikes downward,
brakes it to a murmur.

But that foraging squirrel
scrambling over the slope
has no time for you;
the hunger in his belly
has made him one-track crazy
after food; his twitching tail bobs
goodbye, goodbye, goodbye.

126

The sun, frozen by the clouds,
rolls out to find you
moving across snow-sugared
parched-through lifeless grass,
arrowed toward home;
too late he tempts you
to follow him over
the next hill and the next.
Perhaps tomorrow, you tell him,
and he understands—or seems to,
for he at least smiles down
morning's first warming
golden benediction.

JOURNEY

Single drops of water
with a shine of white

take the ski-tow slide
down the day's rusty clothesline.

127

INTO NIGHT

As you walk out deep into night
feel how the trees are leaning over
to watch you on your way.

Hear dead leaves hiss and crackle
as you twist them underfoot,
as winds whip and shuffle them.

See how each streetlight plays
at being the ultimate
all-too-solemn moon.

Sense that all lighted houses
stand ready, each one waiting
your firm knock on the door.

Know without lifting your eyes
one star up there will burn
brighter than the rest for you.

KENSINGTON MARKET

Nothing here says
you have to buy even a dime's worth.

But even if you have to hold your nose,
shove your head into the near dark
of a few side-street stores.

Examine fruits and vegetables
as you would the breasts of a woman
taken to bed for the first time.

Handle warily the yard-wide
caballero's hat
which the label claims Madeira-made—
then admit with a smile
that it hides too much of your eyes.

Above all, remember each smell,
each new sensation
that this hot day offers you,
remember, too, how these people sweat to please.

And if you feel like a little lie
tell your friends: I had a squid
brained to order at Kensington Market—
they may almost believe you. . . .

KITE

Man and daughter
boldly voyaging their kite
high out above the river.

Doling out string
with much patience
as the kite madly signals them,
feeling his wings.

Haven't they heard
that kites become crazed,
go mad with alternatives,
hovering between clouds
and flashing-by water?

If there was time
I'd run to warn them,
but all I can do now
is watch, stricken dumb,

as, almost when it seems
their golden bird's hooked fast
to playtime winds,
tail a swirling thing,

it staggers, then plunges
surprised as down a well
to the phlegm-ugly rocks,
to the stupid waters,

where it lies there crushed,
river-soaked, torn forever,
gay dancer of the upwinds
sudden prey to strange forces,
fatal earth fascinations.

MOVING DAY

Seventeen years
on the same street,
seventeen years
in the same house.

Now that we go
how much of this street,
of this house
will go with us?

As much as we care to take,
as much joy or heartbreak
as we have room for.

131

NIGHT OVER HURON

Lake fishermen
hardly use this port anymore.
Nothing much in these waters
but the corpse-stink of fish.

That one bell-buoy out there
says it all as it rings out
its steady keening whine,
shivering the air as the light slides,

as night creeps in, reverberating
lonely and lost
over all this great dark,
flooding emptiness.

132

THE LEAF MAN

(For Susi)

When October winds
tug the panic sleeves
of each tree and down
the crowded leaves slip and slide,

see the old man who labours
in our neighbourhood
with his clever machine
to stitch them back on trees,
with his brush to paint them
dreamiest of summer greens;

his uppermost thought
to keep winter away
one last time before
his staples reach their end,
his brush runs finally dry.

133

At the Fort, when the news came,
he said little (what was there to say
that those cursed Yankees, first slipping
boldly across the river, then storming
the heights with everything carried
before them, hadn't already spoken?);

but ordered his horse saddled
with the greatest speed, and calling out
to his orderly strode to his room,
where his sword-belt was buckled on
over the immaculate tunic. One quick last look
in the nearby mirror made him flinch
for a moment only—there wasn't the time
to waste this night of all nights
on his mirror's sudden caller,
especially when the fellow sported
amazingly his own likeness, and the bullet-hole
from which the blood seemed to be spurting
all too quickly now
was through the proud, splendid full-dress
of a British general. . . .

134

JAZZMAN

Sometimes he'd like to slip
his blackness on a white man and say,
walk around a while like this,
see how it really feels. . . .

Another time he yearns
to smash both his fists
into that white sneer,
that indifference,
without having to explain
to himself or anyone
the justice of it all.

At another time to laugh
at the whole square world
he no more fits into
than trumpet with Guy Lombardo,
or to cry for no reason
than to counterpoint his joy.

To do all this he takes
a cornet in his hands
to squeeze through, force out
all hate, sickness, fear
from its dazzling end,

pointed high at heaven,
lowered straight at hell.

ON THE ROUGE

I can almost see now
my father's canoe
pointing in from the lake,
him paddling, mother hidden
behind a hat of fifty years ago.

Turning up a narrow stream
clear-flowing through marsh
(not mud-brown like today):

gliding under the same
railway bridge we cross under,
slipping by the same giant
stepping-stones of rock
standing solid as ramparts:

moving on to those quieter
summer-singing reaches,
the busy calling of birds
making speech difficult.

Lost finally, perhaps forever,
behind ferns swallowing up banks,
bent trees overarching sky,

drifting the summer
labyrinths of love.

THE GOOD DOCTOR

(For the memory of Dr. Norman Bethune)

Not one of the women the good doctor charmed in Montreal, London, New York, ten or twenty years before, would now recognize the old man looking seventy in death but in fact only forty-nine—those steel shafts gone from his eyes, that restlessness drained from each nervous muscle.

And how about old patients who had the good doctor's knife slice around their rotted lungs, who never heard the curses that flew, never saw the scalpels hurled to the floor with the nurses in tears; the good doctor they knew (smiling, moustached man with a receding hairline) stopping in late at night to say hello —no, they too wouldn't recognize this death-mask with all the weight of the wounded and dying finally lifted from its shoulders.

And the comrades of Spain—they wouldn't recognize the good doctor either, the one remaining lung motionless at last; blood-poisoning, tiredness and little food having done their work well on the man who only two years before had fought desperately to save the helpless refugees trapped by Franco's pincers on the Malaga road—forty loads a day for three days in the one battered truck, with so many old bewildered ones still left behind to die.

Yes, no-one would recognize this bald, bronzed Canadian, man of the people covered by a white sheet now, his last blood bank delivered, last bandage applied, last appeal for funds typed on the battered portable, last warnings to fat, dead ears delivered with his almost final breath. . . .

Suddenly all these pictures fade—the year becomes 1966, not '39: see Il Caudillo still secure in power, sickeningly fawned upon by all nations; while the treacherous Japanese have become kind and civilized again—overnight it is our friends the Chinese who've become the new monsters.

If the good doctor (coldly locked in a North China grave) is aware of all this he never lets on: instead today he's dreaming of maple trees transformed into colours of autumn, their crimson pouring down the Mountain just like so many years ago— to him the red blood of the people, red flags that wave in joy of victory everywhere.

FUNERAL ORATION

Each time his hand reaches up,
each time his eyes behind their glasses
seem to lose themselves past the ceiling,

I want so badly to tell him
that heaven isn't up that way
on the other side of the roof,

but down here, among us,
living, wherever it can,
in the human heart.

138

SEVEN DAYS OF LOOKING AT A RUBBER PLANT

MONDAY

The rubber plant
in the soiled front window
of the Peacock Hotel
hasn't grown an inch in two years:
which, though it may be a coincidence,
almost certainly dates from the night
it heard the manager complaining
that the way it was mushrooming
it would soon be taller than he was.

TUESDAY

The rubber plant
in the drab front window
of the Peacock Hotel
has conspired with the dust
to form secret tentacles
that wait with patience
the first unsuspecting arm
to show with a duster.

WEDNESDAY

The rubber plant
in the stained front window
of the Peacock Hotel
has suddenly sported
a bright yellow leaf
among twenty of green:
much the same shock to me
as a tall gleaming nude
walking in unannounced
on an annual meeting
of Presbyterians.

THURSDAY

The rubber plant
in the smudged front window
of the Peacock Hotel,
is, I see now,
not one but two.

And I can't blame this
on my eyes as much
as this too-ordered mind of mine,
trying desperately to bring
strength and unity where
neither really can be.

FRIDAY

The rubber plant
in the darkened front window
of the Peacock Hotel
has shivered all day
not so much from the cold,
which is on the outside,
as from the one
new guest of the week,
who has sat all day
hunched under the lightbulb
in the middle of the lobby
with his back to the window,
and hasn't given out
with the warmth of a word.

SATURDAY

The rubber plant
in the sleepy front window
of the Peacock Hotel
often wishes it could shine
like the new chrome chairs
in the outer lobby.

But all it gets now,
year after year,
is the same dull green leaves
and repeated instructions
to grow like a giant
and cover the world.

141

SUNDAY

The rubber plant
in the plain front window
of the Peacock Hotel
has become two legs,
one trying to escape
through the back door,
the other hoping somehow
to make it out the front.

NIGHT RAIDER

Something getting its Christmas dinner early
in the narrow alley flanking our apartment house.

Gorging so frantically it can't hear the noise it makes
rattling trash-can lids, ripping skins
of newspaper-wrapping off the choicest refuse.

All this to the sleepy steadiness of rain falling,
so that I get a picture of my animal,
head down in garbage, busy, steam ascending
like grace from its breathing coat.

SO EASY TO EXPLAIN

So easy to explain
why I followed him all the way over
to Bay Street just to be sure
he found the bus terminal. . . .

There for a moment as he stood
almost helpless at Dundas and Yonge,
blaze of noon slicing through at his eyes
still bandaged from the hospital—

I was that man standing there
waiting for a voice to speak,
waiting for a hand held out,

I was that bewildered man
soaked in the sweat of my fear,
sunshine striking hard at my face
but blackness, darkness pushing all around. . . .

THE WHITE BEDSHEET

Hung up with pride
this election morning,
the whitest and best
of the polling lady's bedsheets.

And I go behind it
to mark down my **X**,
my voice in Parliament,

knowing very well
there's just that laughable
thin, separating screen

between me and all those
who would jackboot my brain,

who would like to lead me,
monkey on their tight-pulled chain,

who could never allow me
this too-personal act
behind the white bedsheet
of the polling-booth lady.

THE RITES

No leaf should be allowed
to cling to any branch
after today.

They should stumble on the ground,
be lifted, flung along
in the circling air.

Each tree must bare itself
to receive the first
stinging lash of winter.

No other eyes may watch
as the crisp blows fall.

That must be a most secret
laying on of agony.

BEYOND

Ahead of me,
branching out from this path,
a new one begins,
slender thread climbing steep
to curve off among trees.

Everything in me cautions:
keep straight to the well-worn trail
which can't lead you too far wrong.

But I find myself shedding all doubts
in the way my back bends
to take the rough tilt of the hill,
by the way my muscles strain
up near the top—all of me so eager
for what lies beyond.

AT THE AIRPORT

Paper handkerchief or silk
it's how you wave
that puts the kiss in goodbye.

146

THAW

From tight-strapped listening
to clock hands night after night,
feeling the oil-less movement
of taut springs coiled around nerve-ends:

to wake at morning to the slow
cunning artlessness of drops
leaking from torn eaves down all the way
to sound's first beginning—
water chafing the unexpected
stubborn roughness of earth.

CAN IT BE?

Can it be
that death is still
nothing more, nothing less
than the choking scent
of flowers draped
around Thelma's coffin
in that parlour room,

desolate but full
of foreboding evil
to the young boy who stood
breathing deeply in and out
to try to slow the panic
mounting, swallowing his heart?

CRAZY SPRING SONG

I'm hemmed in, surrounded,
taken prisoner by greenness.

Each bud-burst in the dark
thrusts through my heart.

Even Death, the Defeated One,
finds himself choking
on too many mouthfuls
of fresh-tasting leaves.

1944

Because we couldn't boot
your Civil Service backside
(nightly battle-ground
of our flight-lieutenant),

we lay sleepless at night
plotting secret missions
for hard-pressed Hitler,
then finally dozed off

into the splendid dream
of Sturmbannführers
raping you to drum-rolls,
to bugles blaring.

MAPLE

How much of magic
still lies between

first-sipped rain
and the soon-to-follow

branch-shy showing
of the buds?

THE WALL

A blind man's walking up this wall
though his cane keeps telling him No,
a blind man's finally been trapped
in this endless maze called the city.

(From now on the blind will wear wings
to glide over us who pass them by
on the street as quickly as possible,
who leave them to tap against a wall
or dare the nightmare navigation
of roadways and sidewalks)—

A girl finally goes to the blind man's rescue,
leads him slowly away from that wall
which some day is waiting for each of us
on a morning as innocent as this one.

TWIN SITTINGS

(Parliamentary Flag Debate, 1964)

The stench is unbearable
in this country outhouse,
the stuff piled closer to the seats
than I've ever seen it before.

Which serves to remind me
this September afternoon,
not twenty miles away
Parliament still sits and sits and sits. . . .

150

THICKSON'S

Spin-tailed swallows
(or whatever)
here by the hundreds,
strung out in bobbing file
on the telephone wires,
thinking already, you say,
of the southward journey.

A cool wind freshens in
off Lake Ontario.

A good day, Ron,
to dust off our wings,
try to fly again,

before autumn slips in
the way it always does,
before the birds leave
another year without us.

UNADULTERATED POETRY

Unadulterated poetry
magically begins to happen
at King and Bay as the four ditch-diggers
slowly converge on the sparrow
who's lost all power in his wings
but a last desperate flutter
that can't keep him long away
from the hairy, huge
meat-hook of a hand,
which, cupped for a moment,
is his prison—

but now becomes (the miracle!)
a warm-beating, soft cell of skin
whose other name is love.

STOPPING BY THE SIDE OF THE ROAD

Brightest, warmest
colour of the day,

this steaming lemon-yellow
corkscrewing snow!

152

MILK-CHOCOLATE GIRL

By now it's a wonder
someone hasn't eaten you
ounce by delicious ounce,
milk-chocolate girl.

Taken already
in very small bites
the slightly snub nose,
the breasts still asleep,
the awakening hips,
the legs very firm.

We thank God you're still
very much in one piece,
to light up the darkness
of this lunch hour for us
with a turn of your head,
a single flash from your eyes.

O easily the most
awkward (still charming) thing
you'll ever do in your life—
the way you're attacking
that slice of bread now!

153

THE HOUSE ON INDIAN ROAD

Tar still drips
on hot days from the roof,
makes black patches on the walk
that, squeezed between board fence and north wall,
comes out on a garden with two trees,
one a cherry, one a peach,
lost among the flowers and vegetable rows.

But that hazel-eyed boy
no longer rounds the corner of the street
on his tricycle and turns up
a walk still strewn with magnolia petals—

grown much older, that boy
no longer cuts the front grass
or clips at the garden edges,
doesn't kneel on the rug
of the upstairs sitting-room,
fingering volumes from the roll-back,
thick, glass-protected book-shelves,
Resurrection by Count Leo Tolstoi,
The Girl's Own Paper
years 1898, 1899,
musty pages picturing long-skirted girls
playing field hockey or grouped
about their form mistress:

no, he doesn't sit in that kitchen
with two gentle ladies
eating summer salad
with a taste of fresh earth
almost clinging to the lettuce
and radishes; and after,
with his eyes lighting up,
doesn't watch the rich, homemade sherbet
spooned from its serving-tray
into a wide dessert dish
set in front of him:

no, that boy doesn't go there any more,
the dear ones he knew have all gone,
strangers sit in those rooms,
walk across those floors,
cut the grass and work that garden.

When he strolls by
it's as a man of a new time,
the years pressing him down;
and when he finally stops
it's around the corner,
safely out of sight,
where tears that well over
are secret and sting
before they're wiped away forever.

NEWS OF THE DAY

After the large cold orange juice,
and halfway through the cereal,
to hear the jabbering
impassive voice of the radio:
two-year-old boy
dead on arrival,
badly dehydrated,
severe malnutrition,
with his brother also
in very serious condition,
both living neglected
on Wellington West. . . .

The slam you give
the refrigerator door
doesn't seem to help at all.

NOBODY'S TOLD THE BIRDS

Nobody's told the birds
that this house has been sold to the wreckers,
nobody's told the birds
that the creepers on the north wall that hide
their nests from the squirrels will die
along with the wall they cling to,
as the crowbars stab brick by brick,
as the bulldozer panzers level off
stubborn stone to a joyless rubble.

Nobody's told the birds,
so they sing on day after day,
and no doubt will be singing the hour
that the crowbars pierce their last brick,
that the bulldozer cuts its hacking cough.
That song will follow right along
to the next house, the next and the next,
a loud song of gladness and light.

Nobody's told the birds,
so that song will go on forever.

157

MONTREAL '65

Across Dorchester Street
an Air Force band plays martially,
puffing the square up into trumpets
to the flow of lovers walking
down rows of paintings exhibition-hung.

(And I thinking gloomily
of what time and this Montreal
has done to both your faces—
laughing, girl-fresh faces
of '42, '43,
now marble-cold,
now tic-twitching,
years closer to death than to life—)

The band bursts through
on a rising surge of brass and cymbal:
lost forever those golden days, whirling times.
Today's chilled glances
write the tragedy of torn loves, dead loves,
nights unending.

I think Burns up there on his statue
might swear beautifully if allowed.

O Canada
comes slowly from the bandstand,
and clinching it, *the Queen.*

COMPENSATION

(For Victor and Elizabeth)

We never did manage that corn-roast
on Ward's Island beach (my dream of it the lighthouse
on Eastern Gap's pier-end answering in flashes
the orange-red magnificence
of our bonfire fanned by wind-bellows
and bent on shattering all darkness. . . .)

But still we had that perfect afternoon
of soft-shaking ferry-floor under us,
of sailboats small and nervous
on the big blow and chop of the bay;
of volleyball down at the beach's edge,
the girls eager, awkward prima donnas,
with each smash shot just out of reach;
of football on the sand, our winner
a six-year-old plunging fullback:

then at last a dock-side wait
(day's slowly sinking matador
taking one last bleeding wound
from the sharp-horned dig of the skyline);
with the island bedding down behind us
to its twin song of willows and water.

AIR-RAID PRACTICE

Tonight when those siren-calls
woke all the neighbourhood,
suddenly memory flooded back
to a far desperate time's
blacked-out wail. . . .

A witch's eve
nightmarishly reborn,
with rifles grabbed,
even bayonets fixed
to cries re-echoing.

Long-dead years
no-one cares about
or even recalls,
but still part of me,
precious for all their waste,
still loved for all their pain.

Tonight when the sirens
woke all the neighbourhood
I stood at this door
and shook for remembering.

A WALK IN THE PARK

A bird sat in a tree
well hidden, and sent
his unwavering lament
out and away from me,

to be answered by another
tone for tone,
sadness for sadness alone.

The road curved down and down.
Footsteps of others in the snow
told me the way I must go on.

BUS-STOP

Alone at the bus-stop
the Japanese mask
of your face reveals
neither joy nor sorrow.

Beautiful mask.
Lonely hour.

A PICKER OF DANDELIONS

Almost unnoticed because the street
jogs madly here,

a middle-aged woman
(heavy-coated to keep out the heat?)
bends well down
between the abandoned ties
of railway track,
where dandelions have rioted,
swarmed over.

One hand plucking golden heads
to drop them lovingly
into a paper shopping-bag,

where pressed down tight
then tighter,
they mesh and mix sweetness,

starting up those sugars
of the holy sun
on their marriage of magic
with the joyous bottles
of gloom-heavy winter.

BOCCE PLAYERS, SEPTEMBER

The moon's out to help
the *bocce* players tonight,
but all they really need
is the one light thrown
from the school's second storey
to the tennis-court below,

where these friends, these neighbours,
take wondrous, impossible shots,
coax lovingly clicking balls,
four shadowed figures caught
and held in the darkness,
not wanting to start what they know
will be the last game of the year.

"Marry a *bocce* player
and see him only
when the snow falls."

Maybe the Italians
never had this saying.
Well, they have it now.

163

AT THE POLANYIS'

(In memoriam Karl Polanyi, and for Ilona)

How did you manage here
all these years,
you, Karl,
you, Ilona,
winter after winter
in a summer cottage?

A couple of stoves,
a mysterious furnace
somewhere in the basement
throwing off at best
illusions of real heat;

with water to be carried
every day from a well
halfway down the steep
slippery plunge to the river,
with often ice to break
before drawing it in winter.

164

And Karl,
I've seen your tiny room.
No desk, they tell me,
so you either wrote
sitting up on your bed,
or used the arm
of your one leather chair;
no space for books,
no fancy filing-cabinets.
And you, Ilona,
with only a cubby-hole
not much better to work in.

But the things you've both done,
what managed to get written,
transmitted or spoken here,
the minds you've helped shape,
the directions you've charted!

Revolutionaries both
of the mind and the spirit,
comfort I can see
was a useless frill
neither one of you
simply had the time for. . . .

Now today, Ilona,
in talking to your present guest,
Ken tells me something strange
crashed against the side of the house
only last night, hard enough
to even shake one of the walls,
and this morning he found
a strange bird close to death
on the front grass—it seems he'd hit
your house in the darkness.

And I thought right away of you, Karl,
coming back perhaps from the other side
to see your Ilona once again
at this piece of ground become
eternally your own:

and quite easily losing your way
in the black shadows of the valley,
but reckless to be back,
risking everything in a low swoop
that failed, but still had
the same breathless reaching-out,
which, knowing no defeat,
scrapes the very stars in its daring!

BOLDT'S CASTLE

The ruins of the castle,
abandoned, half-finished,
are no sadder to me
than each sunfish that toys
with the garbage tourists toss
into the dockside's tepid water.
Both are long-term prisoners
of this island, this river,
island with its grotesque gingerbread
of Rhinish castle,
river with its thousand islands
strung out, bewildering maze
without real beginning or end.

Boldt, so the story goes,
began construction of this castle
as a wedding-present for his bride;
but death took her voyaging
before she even had the chance
to set eyes on it.

No further work was done.
The rooms remain unfinished,
the walls worked over
by time, sun and rain
begin to crumble. The broken dream
of the young German immigrant
come to New York to make his fortune,
sits here now to impress or start a smile.

Another New World dream
begun with power and careless wealth
ending in ruin, in sorrow.
As if a man had no business to let
his imagination soar too grandly;
as if a conspiracy of forces
lurked in the wings, calmly waiting
to bring the curtain down on tragedy:
as if the island finally chosen
to house this fantasy had from the first
hated the honour, while the great river
sliding lordly by had felt the same way,
so both schemed together
how to bring this upstart down,
how to ensure laughter
would never ring in these rooms,
life never flow on these staircases,
boats never dock with their carefree passengers
to people these battlements. . . .

Well, they had their way
or something had its way.
I stand on this wharf now
ignoring the sunfish, deaf to the hum
from the souvenir shop, counting the minutes
before I crowd back on the Rockport launch
with my fellow sightseers, to circle back
through more island mazes, with our driver
giving us the highlights in his sideshow manner;

with the castle far behind us then,
the ghosts all alone now to watch
the sun striking walls with no glass
in their hundred windows to throw back the flames.

Heart Island, Thousand Islands, 1964

168

THE BUD

All this flowering's nothing,
really nothing to me—

it's the about-to-break
look of the bud,
a promise of sudden
burst-out from dark
into light,
into dazzling sunshine.

And then you wonder:
could a life too
be as suddenly reborn?

169

BUTTERFLY ON MELINDA STREET

Butterfly in October
on Melinda Street,

where are you going,
where did you come from?

But it seems
you haven't any time
to answer questions,

as, turning at Jordan,
you flit-flutter up
past the third-storey windows

to do the golden dance
of the morning sun.

170

THE CRY

In the third small hour
from our roof overhead
an almost human cry
of bird or animal.

I closed the window hard
against that unearthly scream,
then stood hard-rooted there
until the wail died away,
freeing blood to run smoothly again,
ears to rewind quietness.

After that went back to bed,
finding all too soon the sleep
of the righteous and the just,

while for all I knew
something up on the roof
still waited an answer
to its desperate cry.

MIGRATION

The same fatal urge that drives me
again and again to your lips,
that flings, then crushes me against your body,

must be something of the same sweet curse
that sweeps the birds up from the golden South
each false springtime of March or early April,
catching them on their unsuspecting flights
at the edge of Erie, Michigan, Ontario,
in a devil's vortex of winds and piercing snow.

So that the shoreline's littered, the waters ride
with ten thousand corpses offered to the grinning gods—
while all my flights,
once they surmount the storms tossed about your thighs,
soar to sun's fire, stars' farthest thrusting,
bringing me hard tossed but joy-swooping back to earth.

THE IMMIGRANT

(For Jozo)

Each face has two ears
tuned-up deaf to catch
each stumble of my speech,
two eyebrows to lift
at the clothing I wear,
two lips to form a sneer
at the house where I live.

Yet it's useless to hate
as my heart says I should,
for I must swallow pride
to ape everything they do,
somehow make myself over
into one of them,
or end up a nothingness,
not having learned
there's only one way up
for those such as me—
death and final burial
of the man I once was.

Only then will these masks lift,
faces hold out their hands.

THE FARM OUT THE SYDENHAM ROAD

(For Joan, who invited us)

1. DIRECTIONS

"Turn off No. 2
at the Sydenham Road,
go north two miles
past the 401,
watch out at the top
of the second hill for a sign:
O. R. ORSER
PRODUCER OF BEE-MAID HONEY:
that's your home away from home."

2. THE HOUSE

Much more than you expect to find
at the end of a bone-jabbing
excuse for a lane
in off smooth highway.
Trees that surround it
seem to stretch, to climb up the dark
as our high beams stab at them.
As if with any luck
these strangers won't see the house
behind this screen of leaves,
will turn and go away. . . .

174

The single bulb burning
in the lawn-light breaks
the tight shield of blackness,
and we see the fieldstone front
for the first time,
fall in love with it right away.

But it's not love this house is after,
survival's more. Simply to remain,
to add more years to a century and a quarter
of slow-paced living
through a new time frightening in its speed,
its contempt for the old,
so ready with wrecking-bar, wrecking-ball
and bulldozer for any obstacle
pride, stubbornness strews in its way.

See the house in daylight,
watch how it blends with this land,
sits here as naturally belonging in the middle
of fields burned by the sun
the same colour as its walls.

Compare it with the bungalows,
the split-levels building a mile below—
red-bricked, deadly functional,
looking almost as if lowered
from the air onto alien ground,
not even the games of children
able to make them come alive.

I give you two,
three years at the most, old house,
so draw out each day
each night to full savour,
carry snow on your roof with new grace,
take the beat of rain as gentle chiding,
endure sunstroke of early August
with dignity, be tolerant even
of these strangers now under your eaves
for the next three days.

3. RABBIT

Brown rabbit caught in our headlights
shows neither speed nor interest
in leaving through the tangled ruins
of raspberry bushes.

4. THE ORCHARD

Bees and butterflies
make their casual, sun-soaked sorties
from one swollen
thistle's lip to another,
oblivious of the deliberate metronome
of apple after apple
gently thudding into the parched
desolation of the August grass.

176

5. TREES AROUND THE HOUSE

When the land's finally surrendered
to row-on-row suburbia,
these trees will be the first to go
and a thousand birds with them,
and ten thousand birdcalls
and at least ten
perfect morning choristers.

6. CICADAS

As the heat stabs deeper
so the cicada's torment
winds and unwinds
around trunks and branches
of these trees, which surround
and hide us from the road.

7. COWS OF CATARAQUI

Cows of our neighbour
look so hostile at me
I become a gladiator
on his first fight in Rome
looking up in awe
at the blood-loving Coliseum crowds.

8. THE CREEK

The creek's bone dry,
and the cattle that come here
to sit in the shade
and find they can't get a drink
in between munchings,
have piled its rocky bed
with fly-swarming dung
to show their disgust.

9. CROW

Just when you'd welcome
his coarse laugh he's silent
as his namesake the scarecrow;
then, when it's neither
time nor place for his mockery,
out it comes, high from the lookout
of some mysterious tree.

10. THE BARN

The old barn torn down,
shattered for the sake
of the great pine timbers
that held it aloft
a hundred years and more.
Along with the twisted, bleached
scatterings of snake fence,
these discarded planks make
of slow rot a muted
patient suffering.

11. THE PASTURE

Baked dry by sun
lanced through by wind,
cropped just short of death
by the long-tailed herd,
the pasture suffers my presence,
sends only a startled
grasshopper up,
sweats and chokes in its dust,
dreaming of greenness
in another spring.

12. CRICKETS

Last thing we hear
between love and sleeping,
as if to tell us
long after our leaving,
night pulsates on
through the living darkness.

13. THE BELLS

Three copper bells
tied to some string
hanging near the door-knob,

ring silver all hours,
but clearest, most tingling,
in hoot owl's first
yellow hour awake.

14. EPITAPH

Mornings I'm no longer stirring,
I, Orville Orser, beekeeper,
my bees gone in a cloud, whirring
up so like death's last blur.

HURDY-GURDY IN THE SNOW

Monkeyless,
no-one turning the crank,
not one note of music unwound.

Restaurant and Tavern
printed boldly
over the undercoat of cream.

Sitting out in the snow looking worse
than an abandoned ice-box.

Why didn't you have the courage
to smash it to bits the first day,
Mr. Pepio?

THE SNOWS OF SUMMER

Long released now
from winter's hold,
I can even smile
at our snow-ball bushes
littering the drive
with petals the same
idiot white that those
perpetual storm skies
sifted through and down,
aching then the eye
and blinding all
but the most stubborn mind.

THE SIRENS

Though you may escape them,
bound tight to the mast,
ears well plugged,
sight the one betrayer—

some day, when least expected,
you'll hear that singing
(grown more compelling, you can only guess),
note every gesture eyes once telegraphed
from that forbidden shore
(now at the moment of the writhing climax),

and know your good captain lied,
that his ropes and wax
did you only disservice:
that all your life you'll hear
those mocking, taunting voices,
see those bodies sinuously beckoning,
insidious by day, tumultuous by night.

182

SPRING SOAKING

Pelting my hair,
sluicing down my face,
juicing at my lips—

after winter's five
grey-black-white Inquisitions,

to find myself drowned
in the warm and gentle
rain-bath of spring!

THE WORM

Don't ask me how he managed
to corkscrew his way
through the King Street pavement,
I'll leave that to you.

All I know is,
there he was,
circling, uncoiling
his shining three inches,

wiggling all ten toes
as the warm rain fell
in that dark morning street
of early April.

183

I LIKE TO IMAGINE

I like to imagine
that the tip-tap-tap
of the blind man's cane
down this side of the street,

somehow beats the time
for the young legs racing
up the other.

BILL

All day long I've tried
to recall your face,
this through the time-block
of twenty years and more. . . .

And this evening
it finally comes to me—

now I know
(and no better for it)
that after $16\frac{1}{2}$ kills,
the DSO, DFC and Bar,

the biggest, brawliest
(curly-headed) kid
in our high school

went for his.

THE MARRIAGE BIT

The sudden mad blasting
of horns from the cars
in the wedding procession
now gliding by the house,

almost drowns out the way
they are standing in the kitchen
screaming screaming at each other.

NEVER LOOK BACK

Of all times to come along this street
and see my old school in its last crumbling days
under the wreckers' crowbars!

Never look back—
the danger's always lurking.

Something or someone wants me
to end up like Humpty,
swaying first, then sliding off,
to fall, so finally, shatteringly down!

THE LAST PIECE OF BREAD

A starling comes down
for the last piece of bread,
beaks it, then flies up
toward the roof-top behind,
then halfway across lets it fall,
but wings on, not breaking flight.

Who could say it wasn't pride or anger
made him show no sign of his loss?

Or even a code that says:
when you aim your wings
go there swerveless, unwavering?

HOW NATURAL IS GAS

To the radio's hundred
sobbing, oversweet strings,

he is stuffing newspapers
into those wide leering
mouths beneath doors,
and around the unsmiling
licked-dry windows' lips.

WEEPING WILLOW, EARLY SPRING

Filigreed
strange green
tresses of a girl

tossed about
overflowing

the mean
slightly crooked
stilt-trunk of a tree.

NIGHT WITH SLOW FREIGHTS

Slow freights
and none-too-slow freights
rail-tripping through a night
hung down with rain sounds
grown huge, magnified beyond
all daylight proportions.

Underneath it sleep
becomes a hollow drum
on which insistent drops
go hush-like, tom-tom heavy. . . .

RED ROSES ON THE TRELLIS

Within those warm
moist places of the dark,

colourless,
only the tentacles
of their perfume reaching out,

red roses on the trellis
lewdly french-kissing night.

FUNERAL DIRECTOR

When the Reverend at graveside
shouting over the wind,
reaches the appropriate words
on his flapping Bible page,

very deliberately your hand
sprinkles just the right amount
of fine brown sand
in the form of a cross
on the shiny coffin top,

then just as deliberately
returns to your leather glove,
before the January wind
now spearing the snow crust
turns and snaps your fingers off.

WASP NEST

(For Frank and Marion)

The wasps at the north end of your verandah
have the best view of Lake Massawippi
three terraces below.

So easy to get rid of them,
you say, a paper bag
suddenly popped over the nest
would do it. But there's a fascination
in watching the work expand
inch by inch as the weeks slide by,
seeing another form of life go about
its living with a frenzied earnestness
a dedication to shame us listless humans.
What if one gets careless sometimes
and draws a sting or two?
Can you really blame these home-loving buzzers?
Think of them, if you will,
as *les séparatistes* of North Hatley,
better tolerated than stirred up,
better at the end of the verandah
in plain view than hidden in the woods. . . .

And who knows, in time
we may even come to know each other
well enough to live together
under this same good roof.

THE PRAYER AND A SACRILEGE

1

Christ on your spire,
guide of all good mariners,
point the one way from ship
up the dark unending streets
to climb at last that Mountain
where all journeys end.

2

A sacrilege perhaps,
but the finger of Christ
points straight from his pedestal
on the Church of the Sailors
down history-crawling streets
to Joe Beef's, the oldest
loudest tavern in town.

SAY GOODBYE

Say goodbye to our neighbours.

Those who through the years greeted us,
laughed with us, quarreled with us,
endured our arguments,
shivered through our screaming,
exchanged light words
on back steps in summer,
in spring over fences.

So as we drive away,
wave to them, those who were there
to be close to,
that now as the car jerks ahead
we look back at,

faces never really known,
the familiar, so-agreeable strangers.

JOHN SUTHERLAND, 1919–56

On my first Air Force leave, '42,
we met. Summer squirmed over Montreal
as we lugged cold quarts of *la bière Frontenac*
from Marcus' Milton Street Clip Joint,

"Smallest Hole in Town Where the Customer is Always
    Wrong,"
back to your Durocher Street apartment
where your bride of three months looked far too radiant
for any one man. That night at the Blue Bird

my new friend Louis to the throb of violins
undertook to teach me poetry. I barely made
the Ocean Limited at twelve, let it hurl me East Coastwards,
blur of blue-flamed streets left behind lighting up my berth.

While bursts of our forty-fives shivered
against the armament-section's test wall,
I read *First Statement*, your magazine now kindling
a war back in Montreal more cold-blooded

than the Coventry razing, more ruthless
than a Commando raid. All this seemed far away
to me on Cape Breton Island, then even more remote
in Yorkshire the next year. When I came back to Montreal

the war was over, your fighting nearly over too.
I walked with you up that Craig Street lane
to your "office," kicking garbage and stray cats
out of our way. Rebellion had cost you

already too dearly, the scars running deeper
couldn't be laughed off any longer.
You'd learned what all of us have, before or since,
that Art is the Iron Whore, asking all, giving little in return.

So I wasn't that surprised when you came,
fiery-converted RC, to Toronto
nine years later (ex-McGill student now at St. Mike's
on the slenderest of shoe-strings),

though I listened amazed one evening
while waiting at your place for supper,
as you extolled the hierarchy of angels
then switched in the next breath to Roy Campbell's greatness

with none of your old oaths, old cynicism
to make it sparkle as before. You were hooked, all right, but I
    didn't mind
if that was what you really needed. And I suppose it was,
that and your wife's unflinching love, for the time ahead.

As of that moment you had something less
than two years to live. . . . One Sunday the four of us sailed
across the Lake to Queenston, drank beer in Niagara Falls, NY,
sent postcards reporting the mythical

Goat Island Conference For an End to Poetry
to some friends, a few enemies; froze that night
on the *Cayuga*'s upper deck as the unfriendly night winds
chilled and re-chilled us. It was only the next month

I found you out at Weston's infamous San,
grinning up at me from bed as one well seasoned
conspirator to another. You swallowed twenty pills in relays
and we got back to writing talk. Six long weeks later

you'd had enough of sanatoriums, walked out to Forty-Nine
    Sussex.
From then it didn't seem any time at all
to that over-white, too-antiseptic room looking down
on University Avenue's mad-dog traffic,

only you couldn't see it, flat on your back (for alternate
    half-hours anyway),
watching TV on a mirror hung up above you,
drowsing, when the pain let up between
    flip-overs, to the endless clack-clatter
of the air-conditioner your father'd had installed

to fight the swarming summer heat. I recall too vividly
the Stryker Frame issue of your review, then that original
strange book on Pratt rushed non-stop through Ryerson Press
just so you'd hold a copy in your own hands in time,

and the poems, your first in years, somehow squeezed out
in those precious last weeks. Then that other half of the body
still living, still vibrant, chickned out on the brain,
the unconquered spirit. I went to see you, John,

at the funeral parlour, had you all to myself
for ten whole minutes, but there wasn't anything more to say
that we hadn't said already. I went out again
into the pitiless heat, back into that world

you'd finally fled from. . . . Writing this now so many years
    later,
I know far too well what a small legacy you've left,
how much your name's been forgotten. It's high time I said
what I've waited so long to say.

194

A CHRIST ON YONGE STREET

The same long hair, same beard,
same gentle eyes.

His back to Yonge Street
he is smashing both fists
against a wall.

But not hard enough to draw blood,
so of course no-one notices.

195

ON OUR FIRST DAY OF MAY

On our first day of May
this bomb that's the sun
is smashed in our faces.

Explodes, blows to bits
any cancer in our hearts,
explodes, shoots to hell
any meanness in our eyes,
explodes and blasts forever
all death smell on the earth.

On our first day of May
this bomb that's the sun
shatters everything evil
in one golden mushrooming
sky-burst of love!

THE FIRST SCARLET TANAGER

Lightning's wildest flash
tamed to flame-flutter,

fires today the murmurous
green of my poplar tree.

196

Lost & Found
(1968)

A SHADOW

A shadow should be
a comfort, a companion,
especially on cold winter nights.

Mine's neither,
being more of a nuisance,
either playing at stepping on my heels,
or making like terror, fond of showing
blackness so close behind
darker than anything I've seen
even deepest in myself.

THE VISIT

White-haired, wrinkle-worn,
my mother, my father wave after us
as we drive away;

not sad yet not smiling,
as if at last
they were used to farewells.

But not me, their son.
I weep unashamed
as the thought wells over:

one day they'll not be here
to say goodbye!

THE INTERRUPTION

The cool breeze at the window
only gets the attention of the lovers
for three short taps of the blind.

THE BED FROM HOLLAND

This bed you point to,
say you were conceived in,
firmly-built, old-world beautiful—

the same, say your eyes,
my new love will be
from her first time turning
in all whiteness there.

199

HALLELUJAH

A kid at the corner
of Queen and Church
smells of too much wine
with noon only ten minutes gone.

Standing only in shirtsleeves
while I shiver in my coat,
he first tries to hustle
a cigarette, then a dime
"for a cup of coffee,"
half-chanting all the time
"Hallelujah, I'm a bum."

He must see the questioning
look in my eyes—
"Is that so bad?"
he wants to know
with a twinkle in his own.

And I find I can't answer him,
and he knows it,
damn his soul.

PENSIONERS IN THE PARK

Money hardly ever changes hands,
but the players pick up their cards
and arrange them so carefully
you'd think each game was one
they'd waited for all their lives.

In between as the cards are shuffled,
they look away at the grass,
up into trees newly-budded,
watch a boy lead his girl down the path,
still scarcely believing that they sit
at this bench with old cronies
under a pulsating sun and stretching sky.

Far behind them now
the frozen nights, sunless days
of their merciless winter.
Life a thing somehow good,
even precious again.

FOR JOHN POCOCK'S DAUGHTER

Something we had to defend
urged us to war in our time.

Today you find
only rough, patient arms of policemen
to go limp in.

WATERS

Good waters work at,
seek out unceasingly
their own perfect level.

So late this March morning
of sun on the hillsides
with the snow still lingering,

each path's been upgraded
to a running-brook thing,
its beginnings dripping pools
that bulge and pour over
as the slopes slip down,
brake abruptly at bottom.

First waters of spring
now unleashed and feeling
such a childish pleasure
in spilling downhill!

ON THE ISLAND

A strict flight of seagulls
rose, then shattered down the beach.

In the pause that hung
in that turbulence two mallards
with wing-strokes of patience, strength
of all continent-crossers,
arrowed over evening-empty sands,

leaving longed-for summer
which had hardly been,
unmourned, even thankfully over.

(For Elizabeth)

Granted, the most natural thing
in the world—the new baby cries,
the young mother bares her breast
to feed the precious, greedy monster.

Then how to explain my shame
coming on you in the kitchen,
unprepared for the great hanging tit,
the suckling infant. . . .

So that I mutter words, any words,
so that I want almost desperately to drop
the glass of rye and ginger-ale,
to back out, to hide,
anything but raise my eyes. . . .

And I repeat—this thing you do
the most natural in the world.

And now finally know myself
earth's most unnatural,
life's most unprepared fool.
And can't help wondering:
how many of us begin like your infant,
but never really leave the breast, suck at it
all the innocence of our lives?

A WITNESS FROM JEHOVAH

When her eyes lit up
and this daughter of Jehovah
raised her arms, I believed,

and followed close behind her
until we reached
the high-speed elevator,
which rose with us both
up through Babel's tower
to the three-hundredth floor,

from where we watched,
now completely unmoved,
as the world below
went up in sudden flames
in that very thorough
Old Testament way.

WALKING OCTOBER'S STREETS

Walking October's streets through nights
hung with too yellow-sharp a moon.

Hearing how intolerably one leaf
can drag the pavement on its claws.

Feeling the cutting-edge on bone
of last cold cricket's whimpering creak.

THE ROSES

Roses wither,
petals fall
then scatter.

But none wither
scatter more
than us.

DRIFTWOOD

This log belongs neither
to earth nor to water,

but being wood
crouches low on the beach,
holding on
as long as it can
to land.

206

THE WORDS

CHRIST DIED
TO SAVE THE UNGODLY
the sign trumpets down
from the valley's
well-drained rock face.

But with spring
leaf and green-twisting vine will cover
these words of the zealot,

and only after burnt-out autumn
the message again
in all its nakedness

which nobody passing
ever reads.

A SHARING

The pup put out
for his morning airing
gets so charged up
when I fuss with him
that he dribbles over me.

How's that
for a sharing of pure joy?

KILLING A BAT

You don't get rid of a bat
by flushing him swiftly
down the nearest toilet:

he'll swoop and swerve
through your head for days,
a torn-loose piece
of blackest night,

who was perfectly content
before being roused
to rest behind the curtains
of this upstairs room.

But a thing unclean,
unfit to live, to those
who swinging out wildly
with soaked towels, attempt

the one thing instinct
hammers through their heads—
kill him, kill:
while his wings flail the air

in a hopeles effort
to escape, stay alive:
but there's none, he dies,
and they die a little too.

SHOW TIME

With my fifty-foot television tower
giving the clearest picture of all,
I can sit on a foam-rubber chair
and watch their First Air Cavalry
flush out a Viet Cong guerilla, spray him dead
as he breaks for it; zoom in on the faces
of villagers after a shelling as they wait
to have their wounds bandaged;

all the time sipping the ale
that's both lusty and light—
with blood gush, bone crush, shock terror,
even a bomb's shriek or gunfire's whining,
easily adjustable or removed altogether
by a knob's simple turning.

THE SMALL COLOURED STONES

The small coloured stones
you picked on the beach,
then brought home to place
in the plastic tray,

shine, even sparkle
as well as they are able,
away from the grit play
of sand, the slow-tongued
soft honing of water.

WEEPING WILLOW

Nowhere a more
unabashed surrender
to sun and wind.

Response to air delicate
as the most tinkling
shivering Chinese glass.

The stretching out
of a thousand fingers
to clutch the sun's
elusive ball of gold.

Roots reaching down
into their own
seven cities of beginning.

So Far So Good
(1969)

AUGUST GARDEN

Proud tassels of the corn,
peaches heavy on their branches,
roses strung along the fence
now shrunken, more ragged
than our memories.

There, spiralling, shooting up
as if the playtime sun
has his magnet on them,

two plain white butterflies
in a whirling climb
of wings and love,
bewildering the eye
but making the heart
go soaring with them.

HOW TO SKIP STONES ON A ROUGH DAY

No use bringing the arm back
then whipping it out
so that the muscles twang after,

but easy, aiming
across the trough
of the least rebellious wave.

212

CHASING THE PUCK

Viewing shoot-for-the-corner
slap-shot, drop-pass antics
of Hockey Night in Canada—
Leafs versus Red Wings
in Mr. Smythe's well-heated ice-palace,

it's not hard to let the mind wander,
to put skates on twelve-year-old ankles,
to clear ice at Second March and dodge
the tips of wind-whipped bulrushes sticking through;

to find one five-below morning
(spent under echo-booming curve
of Old Mill Bridge) my good right foot
well-frozen, and taking me at least
five minutes' agony with biting snow
rubbed hard and almost through the skin
to bring it redly back....

To come finally to that afternoon
my shot caught their goalie in the eye,
and the game ruined with him turning
away from me after that....

But now Gordie Howe
side-steps, fakes, then moves in,
and I'm right there behind him
poised for the shot, the net-bulge, the electric roar!

AT THE WEDDING PARTY

The little girl
who won't smile for me
though I try every trick I know,

circles once to the beat of the drum,
circles once to the saxophone and trumpet,
circles once to the accordion,

then starts it all over again,
a dizzy, swirling childhood round,
which needs neither sense nor reason
to snare a living beauty all its own,

that could be her three tender years,
or the party dress angel white,
or the shining clasp holding up her hair,

or even the hope that my years ahead
could go whirling with her round and round,
so simply unconcerned, so much at ease,
with all my desperate madness gone at last.

AT THIS MOMENT

At this moment my life
as uncertain as the glitter
of this icicle's tomorrow,

hair-trigger hung
between air and river
on the waterfall's shivering
overlip of ice.

215

TWELVE DAFFODILS AT EASTER

Held to the room's deadened light
you shine so, leap glowing out the window,
make the uncalled-for snow matting branches
unsecure, ripe for falling,
turn a corner of the day to sun,
make the rest of it unworthy.

O you are spring's
secret subterranean fire
kept burning at low flame
in the deep-hearth hollows of your blossoming.

THE UNDERPASS

Under can be
such a mad echo way
of going through.

DOWNTOWN TRAIN

This morning my day's beginning could read like a hundred others—reluctant rising, kiss on the forehead of drowsing wife, gulped breakfast and a twelve-minute walk through shaded side-streets to Keele Station,

where a subway train rattles in on perfect time, where I take my window seat in the almost empty car, where I make myself comfortable and doze off very soon after the trainman blows the second of two piercing blasts on his whistle and the coaches jerk forward,

to suddenly awaken, noticing with a start that I'm all alone in the long, beautifully air-conditioned car, that we don't slow down at all for approaching stations but flash right through—and, for that matter, why shouldn't we?—there's not a single soul waiting on any platform!

Still, the trainman's still aboard somewhere and of course the driver, so I'm not *all* alone—I hear his over-shrill whistle repeated with the same strength time and time again, though I can't tell exactly where he's stationed, and I wonder why he has to whistle at all now that the tunnel's pitch black with no red, green, yellow winking signal-lights ahead, now that we don't rush past station platforms any more, now that we're gathering more and more speed until it seems that the train won't be able to stay on the rails much longer, much longer....

With all the time a warning sign above me flashing on flashing off FOREVER FOREVER FOREVER.

THE FIRST TWO ACORNS

Only the first two acorns
really counted.
The first,
unhitched from a top branch,
plunged relentlessly through
heavy leaf screens (leaving the air
still shivering behind it)
to strike the roadway.
hard enough to hurt.

The second could have fallen
from any height.
All that the night heard
was a dull plop in grass,
unspectacular to say the least
after that first heavy drop.

Still, it was the one triggered off
tree after tree down the street.
And all on a windless night
with everyone asleep
and only I to ponder
what would happen next
and exactly when.

THE SONG

The song the old laundry-man makes
as he shuffles on run-down shoes,
striped laundry bag slung on his back,

is pure Cantonese and could be
just the babbling of a doting mind,
not a clear head's outburst of joy:

perhaps saying nothing more than this—
that again through the buds and the steam
he's walked into another spring!

WALKING THROUGH SACKVILLE

(For Alex Colville)

It's hot, mid-summer 1944.
A friend and I in Air Force blue
are walking through Sackville, along dusty streets,
heading for the highway that with luck will take us
to Amherst and the liquor store
before six-o'clock closing-time.

It's almost three now.
Out past the rushes at the road's edge
we can see across the Tantramar Marshes
for miles and miles and miles.
Unimpressive country to a foreign eye,
and our throats dream of ice-cold beer,

but Alex Colville isn't here yet to ask us in
for a cool bottle. Alex Colville isn't ready yet
to make this summer afternoon come alive
with his palette. Alex Colville at this moment
is still storing up in his mind these streets, this marshland,
he hasn't yet settled on his dogs, his old men, his horses,
his trains, his children. . . .

We finally get a lift at the corner,
and very soon Sackville and its streets are left behind,
which, as it still waits for Alex Colville,
nods off again to sleep
until he is quite ready to begin.

GOOD DOG SAM

Good dog Sam
never plays favourites
especially in election year,

spending equal wetting time
on the original posters
of both the Liberal
and Progressive-Conservative
York-Humber candidates.

WHAT THE CAMERA NEVER CATCHES

(For Denny Spence)

This woman goes by me,
not much more than thirty,
all four arms and legs
wrapped in bandages
(her body too?),

walks by me
in a thin cotton dress
without sleeves,
me shivering steadily
as I walk up and down
these pavements, gaze
into each store-window,
all the time
with the camera eye on me
recording "the poet on Yonge Street,"
"the feel of his city. . . ."

And it suddenly hits me—
she's Yonge Street,
she's this city!

As I watch her she stops
at the corner of Dundas,
crosses west with the light
to the other side
and goes down it,
walking almost majestically
with her bulk
with her bandages
with her nothing face
registering nothing,
only those bare shoulders
that thin cotton dress
making me shiver again

as she fades out of sight.

223

GET THE POEM OUTDOORS

Get the poem outdoors under any pretext,
reach through the open window if you have to, kidnap it right
    off the poet's desk,
then walk the poem in the garden, hold it up among the soft
    yellow garlands of the willow,

command of it no further blackness, no silent cursing at
    midnight, no puny whimpering in the endless small hours,
no more shivering in the cold-storage room of the winter heart,

tell it to sing again, loud and then louder so it brings the whole
    neighbourhood out, but who cares,
ask of it a more human face, a new tenderness, with even the
    sentimental allowed between the hours of nine and five,

then let it go, stranger in a fresh green world, to wander down
    the flowerbeds,
let it go to welcome each bird that lights on the still-barren
    mulberry tree.

POMEGRANATES IN STUDIO ONE

(Another for Louis Dudek)

In the TV studio the poet
has begun to read his poem
"The Pomegranates,"
a fine one, in my book
he hasn't written too many better.

But someone has placed four real (live?) pomegranates
in a coloured bowl, and beside it another bowl
in which two more of the fruit
have been halved, then quartered,
the whole thing sitting on a table now
with spotlights and cameras on it.

Strange how the eyes cut off the words
both my ears strain to hear,
eyes pulling me away
from both poem and poet,
all because of this radiant, natural fact.

Is it because we've grown tired
of too many words, even good ones,
or have we let the eyes
overpower the mind, leaving eyes
too undisciplined?

While I ponder this
and a poet reads on about pomegranates,
the whole barn of a building glows
from those fruited halves, those quarters,
blood-red, bleeding on a table....

LATE ARRIVAL

Someone's always late for every meeting,
especially poetry readings.

Tonight it's a moth
swept in on spring air through the open window
right in the middle of Dennis Lee reading
his third "Civil Elegy": flutters once across the room
so surely, so gaily it takes
all my breath away.

Then as suddenly becomes
some part of this room, like a spot on the wall,
or sits down underneath a chair—

or is it my imagination working overtime?—
changes in the wink of an eye
to the young unspoiled face
of a girl in the front row smiling up at me.

226

WE WERE INNOCENTS THEN

We were innocents then—
no napalm, no air-to-air missiles. . . .

Why, it took a whole week
to kill fifty thousand
at Hamburg, the worst raid
on Tokyo managed
only twenty thousand more,
while in one day and night
the fire-storms of Dresden
could stifle a mere
eighty thousand civilians.

We were truly innocents,
my generation—
though we often killed with relish,
were given medals, called heroes,
and no-one seemed to mind,
not even the Enemy. . . .

BACKWATER

Only fifty yards from the subway,
only fifty yards from killing traffic,

a dead arm of the river,
muddy water quite motionless,

up which at the moment
eight ducks (count them) navigate,

father, mother,
their six young ones,

moving so solemnly,
hardly raising a shadow,

that I jump in my skin
as a sudden panic strikes them,

as they scurry, blending in
with the river-line grasses,

then reassured, continue on
in the same smooth column,

while a beaver touches shore,
side-whiskers showing,

over-load of fresh-cut reeds
firmly between his teeth.

THE CHIMNEY

Lady or Mister Squirrel
who slipped or slithered down
our patched, disused chimney
last week or the week before,

makes desperate clawing,
scratching noises tonight,
while I stand on a chair
and scratch, claw back
a little in return.

But I don't have the urgency
in my signalling that something trapped
in a dark hole and starving slowly
to death must surely have,
couldn't have it.

For me it's just a game
for a few more minutes, then I'll think
of something else to pass the time
and leave off.

There's no way (I tell myself)
for him/her to get through at me,
and the wall's too thick
to let any hint of the smell
of slow death come through.

I scratch back once more.

THE ANGELS

The angels amazed us.

There is darkness here too
they said.

SEND-OFF

I won't have any
fancy mausoleum waiting—
but drawing me up
to old Mount Pleasant
a six-horse prancing
steam-calliope,

its furnace blazing,
its smoke-pipe belching,
as the Maestro at the keyboard
gives out (off-key, then right on)
with a real change chorus
of *Sweet Georgia Brown.*

PITCHING APPLES

Standing in the dead bee-keeper's orchard, morning heat of the sun not great yet, picking up windfalls till I have a handful, then straightening up to throw in my best Columbus Boys' Baseball Club style apple after apple at the gaping hole in the barn's side.

Barn that's hard by the house and collapsing slowly, barn filled high with hay that rots in the dusty silence, barn dying much like this house and the great barn beyond, now nothing more than a few scattered timbers the wreckers couldn't use.

Wonder what he'd say, that bee-keeper, seeing me pitching apples till my right arm aches, bound to get three in a row through the hole or let my arm fall from its socket, stubborn myself as that man to have my way, not counting the cost.

Maybe he'd think me stung silly by his bees, turned a little mad (only his bees went this spring, sold to the highest bidder); maybe he'd just lean back on the rickety snake fence, watching the city boy work out his madness, following the green apples as they streak toward the barn's side, then splatter mostly against the dry wood, pulp of them formed in a pattern of uselessness, juice of them trickling down in a frivolous wasting.

FOR PADRAIG

Someone had smashed
the head off at the neck,
broken one leg and thrown it
down to die, the back broken,
on the river rocks—

some little girl's doll,
a plaything,
now totally abandoned,
so virginally naked:

the whole thing so wrong,
so incomprehensible,
as the voice on the telephone last night
telling me you were dead, Padraig.

BATTERED

My battered Christ
of Yonge Street,
now suddenly old,
more unwashed, more ragged than ever,

shaking so badly
you have to look twice
at the postcard he holds out
to decide it's the same one
he couldn't sell all last week.

THE END OF FEBRUARY

Although this end-
of-February wind
moaning to the eaves' length
in gusts of gloom
doesn't "blow hard enough
to give a gopher the heartburn,"

even the black cat
today hasn't tried
to walk his old footsteps
across the backyard's
zero-crisp snow crust.

GARBAGE IN THE MORNING

The collectors of garbage,
shirts open because of the heat,
bellies bulging over their belts
as they walk down one side of the street,
lifting cans with the slickest movement of the wrist,
taking four to fill the cardboard boxes
they heft up onto their shoulders
and carry to the back of the truck,
where a switch pulled starts into motion
the deliberate, groaning grinder's jaws,
with those boxes of garbage now flipped over
for these hungry metal teeth to go to work on,
to chew, chew, chew. . . .

And look—the prize of the morning!
Some inspired poet of a housewife's
left out a small side of beef
stripped clean of meat in every bleached rib,
on which at least two hundred flies swarm—
a green necklace shining
with a radiance all its own
as the sun glints now and then through the leaves!

THURSDAY NIGHT OUT

The Saints and Sinners
having just left the bandstand,
this may be the best chance we'll ever get—

Louis, you play good accordion,
but I know you've got an urge to try clarinet,
really blow up a storm.

Phyllis, your mother gave you piano lessons,
so you'll be a snap on that off-key piano.

As for myself I've always wanted
to stand up somewhere squarely on my two feet
and make a cornet cry and sparkle like Ruby Braff
(or at least imagine the poetry of doing that),

while I know my wife can hardly hold herself back
from running right up to the drums
and making those sticks start talking voodoo. . . .

So Louis, Phyllis, good wife,
and high-already-on-two-beers bank clerk,
up, up on the bandstand quick and begin
before the short intermission's over.

Make sounds, make any sounds wrong or right,
anything to show we still take breath, feel blood
pulsing through all our veins.
It won't be music to anyone else,
but our own ears will buy it,
which is really the important, the wild thing.

And just imagine the four of us roused enough
to cut at last through the silence,
the small talk, the little dyings inside and around us,
to break out, thrust through into light,
into simple joy and blessed laughter. . . .

See the change in our faces already
in our eyes, the happy glow there:
life turned on suddenly again,
crazily, beautifully right!

PACT

Soon, all too soon,
winter will storm in,
fall heavily on us.

So this very morning
my gnarled, so-bent-over
crab-apple tree and I
have made a very solemn pact.

Until its last red fruit has fallen
we are not defeated,
and will concede nothing.

NATIONAL WAR MEMORIAL

My father could be here,
dressed in whatever
the field-artillery wore—
spurring on his mount
in the six-horse team
that sweat-hauls a 4.5
down a Belgian road

Look of youth on his face,
the youth of a generation
that learned to laugh at death
even when it saw stripped clean
its animal under-face;
youth that endured slime of mud,
rot of damp, scurryings of rats,
asked only the rum ration
warmed by a single candle,
youth that could still eat a meal
after seeing the crushed comrade's face....

How simple their wants!
The perfect dream of all
a week's leave in Paris
with enough franc notes
bulging in their pockets
for cafés and champagne,
for hotels with hot baths
to soak in for hours,
and then after dark
the girls on the boulevards,
très jolies and très chères!

So little their wants!
When they finally came home
it was to a country
so eager to forget
that they found themselves forgotten,
the memories of their battles
fading like the poppies
bought on Armistice Day!

Remember us, they asked,
remember our youth,
our unselfish giving,
remember our dying.

But instead we built them
this fine memorial,
then a thousand more,
and were satisfied,
and did our very best
to bury them all.

CICADA MADNESS

High priest of summer,
with you in your temple
at noon-blaze the world
goes suddenly mad
with the first frenzied wail
of your pipes,
heat-crazed, uncontrolled,
and we begin the shriek
in our heads with you
as the sound goes higher,
higher, higher . . .

then break at the climax,
part slowly on the bed—
writhing, frantic urging over,
charged-up nerve-ends spent—

waiting here in the hot
naked room for your cry
to begin again,
to mock us or anyone
unsure enough to ape
and play at your madness
with a little of our own.

SOME CANADIANS

These, when the first
yellow gas of death came over,
pissed on their handkerchiefs
or ripped-up shirts, stood firm
while the others ran screaming.

This one, when the abandoned
Halifax burned, stood quietly,
saluting the trapped rear-gunner
while his flying suit torched into flame.

Fifty years ago,
twenty-five?
What does it really matter?

Today's indifference, even scorn,
what does it take from their dying,
their daring?
Not honour, not pride,
not love of comrades:

(dead words, hollow phrases
to you of an even
more lost generation)

SHOE-STORE

A good thirty years at least
since the last time I stood in this store,
shy boy of fifteen become forty-five.

Nothing's changed much, except the front
is now a shoe-store complete with fancy mirrors,
theatre folding seats, usual boxes piled
rack after rack to the ceiling.
The shoe repair's well to the back,
separately walled off. In the old days
it was all shoe-making—whirling belts,
gleaming stitchers.

One thing that hasn't changed
is the shoemaker, no more bald
than he was then, stooped a little more
in the shoulders perhaps as he bends
over a buffer, working a pair of lady's pumps
back and forth with complete absorption,
all the long years of skill centred surely
at the ends of his fingers, while I stand waiting quietly
(not wanting to break the spell I've somehow started)
several minutes before he notices me and nods.

Polish immigrant before the War,
hardly able to mouth an English word,
I know he felt alien and lost among us.
All the strength and drive in his body
put to the service of his child,
beautiful girl I scarcely remember,
early a piano virtuoso.

Well, he's prospered since then,
no longer lives above the store.
I wonder if his wife's still alive,
if all goes well with his daughter.

But he wouldn't remember me, so why bother?
Why not leave it all mercifully unknown?

So I ask him simply,
"Can you stitch this up for tomorrow?"
and he answers, "Sure."

I don't ask for a ticket
and he doesn't offer one.
I walk out slowly between his mirrors, shoe-boxes,
close the door on thirty years gone forever.

242

WEEPING WILLOW IN WINTER

Now that I've shattered
the ice riding bare-back
and crystal on your branches,

I try to push you upright,
bend you back from the snow,
my tree, my sleek beauty,

part way up, at least,
the rest I'll leave to you
and your mad desire
to climb and trap the sun
in your shiny branches,

to weave him a crown
of your lady-finger leaves.

243

THE DRESDEN SPECIAL

The RAF called it
the Dresden Special.

Eighty thousand charred bodies
jammed between two bread slices.

But even at that
jolly old Sir Winston
had no trouble lifting it
in his pudgy fingers.

After a bite or two
he smacked his lips, grunting,
Just the way I like Nazis,
very well done....

WAITING FOR RAIN

A good rain
though long in coming;
tongues of the grasses
had stretched themselves frantic
reaching for the heavens.

But something wasn't ready.
There still had to be a day
of death-grey skies
and writhing, listless hours
honed on the crazed cadenzas
of cicadas.

Now a new day
and glorious release!
Bark of trees still drip
from the solid soaking,

but I wait unsatisfied,
hoping for more cool raindrops
to suck between my lips,
to trickle new life down
into my long-parched roots.

245

FULL BLOSSOM

I don't really know
whether one miracle is sure
to beget another—
all I can say for certain
is that this crab-apple tree
had only one branch of blossoms
all last spring: and today, a year later,
every branch is choked with slowly-opening
rose-bud petals of blossoms.

So you'd almost think someone
wished to show us even the most barren thing
may live to be renewed again—if the will hasn't died,
if the patience of earth lives on,
if the love for life hasn't perished—

so may we all take blossom, be renewed,
live even more beautiful again.

VERY SHORT POEM

". . . But only God can make a tree."

(He'll never try it in Sudbury.)

246

"A tiny band of cells
at the base of each stem
loosens and dries out
until it's so brittle
the leaf falls off."

But does it really matter?
They still come down sad.

THE MIRROR

(Betty's Bar, York, England)

For some who chose this mirror
it was their one, their fit memorial.

Drink with me now
to a mad time, a brave time,
to the boys who scrawled their names,

then left here, night after night,
to perish in the sky.

DUCKS, FIVE O'CLOCK, LATE NOVEMBER

Last slant of the day's sun
lighting the murky brown of river water.

On which ducks land
with ripple-drip
of webbed feet trailing.
On which the same ducks
upturn into the same brown water,
ice-cold enough to make
my teeth chatter watching them.

(Or so to feed
each delicious shiver
I imagine it.)

248

ICE VALLEY

The floor of the valley
one great glare-glass
of winter sun!

I slither across ice slabs
not too sure where I walk
is over land or water.

Only one thing's certain—
the river may be buried
but can never die.
No matter how deep
and how slow the trickle,
it flows on somehow
in a numbed silence waiting
for the last shift of ice,
for the first shining, crystal-clear
break-out of water!

THE BIG FREEZE

Half-hypnotized by glazed
crystal drops and gouts of rain
ice-soldered to trees, ears charmed
by click of lacquered branch on branch,

I almost miss the frozen cries
from beneath torn trunks,
flung-down branches, pass casually
agonies of limb, great crushing loads
straining at the edge of death:

finally jarred to my senses,
returned to a savage world
of cruelty, mute suffering
in all things living—
man or these brooding
companions of his solitude,
his trials, his terror.

THE WILD ONE

"Between sets one night
I noticed I was spitting blood
for the first time ever.

I was blowing great
and didn't want to quit,
so I had three quick doubles
to fix things over.

That fixed them *good*.
At the end of the next set
I passed out on the stand.

At the hospital
they couldn't pierce a vein;
had to drill a hole
in one leg to get
a transfusion going.

For a week I rocked back
between life and death,
not caring,
without any pain.

Then one morning
opened up my eyes,
and right away
found myself casing
the nurses going by.

From then on I knew
I had a few choruses
still left to blow. . . ."

And keep blowing them
like you are here tonight,
till hell cools out, Bill!

THE WORM FROM THE CENTRE OF THE WORLD

Seeing the starlings,
beaks down in grass,
heads bobbing as they work
through the soaking rain,

I imagine some bird
getting hooked on a worm
that goes on forever,
a worm that reaches
right down to the centre
of the moist, inner world,

a worm so endless
so sweet to the taste
as mulberries in July,
that he's able to fill
half a million bird bellies
to their ultimate bulging!

THE LAST BATTER

(For Jim Lowell)

Old Luke Hamlin's down there warming up, his baseball cap battered as ever, not looking one day older than he did in the Forties and early Fifties, still with plenty of stuff left—his change-up floating in there slowly enough to count every stitch on the ball, his fast one when it comes digging with a smack into the catcher's glove, his curve a butterfly that can't make up its mind until the very last second the direction it really wants to take.

And Rocky's down there too, Rocky Nelson's on one bent knee in the on-deck circle, working his plug tobacco softer as his two big meat-hooks of hands softly grip three bats, two of which he'll throw toward the bat boy just before taking his ambling, purposeful walk to the batter's box. He also doesn't look a day older than he did all those years he led the League in home runs and runs batted in, besides making put-outs at first look like duck soup, nothing at all.

Now Luke's through his warm-up, saunters out toward the mound. The catcher moves in behind home plate, in a moment will handle the last few pitches before this contest gets under way. Rocky's also up on his feet now, swings his three bats around a couple of times, tosses two away, the time-honoured ritual of discarding the extra lumber, then shuffles up to the plate, very ready for business.

It's a warm afternoon here at Maple Leaf Stadium, a Saturday in late June to be exact. There's a light breeze blowing in off the lake but not enough to bother our players, the sun far enough around so it doesn't shine directly in a batter's eye. Right about now the plate umpire should be yelling "Play ball" and moving back behind the catcher to get set for the first pitch of the game. At this moment the ten to twelve thousand fans in the stands should be breaking out into a minor roar as the first batter stands in there swinging his bat, waiting for the initial delivery. But today there's no umpire dressed in black behind the plate or out behind first or second, and certainly no crowd in the stands—for the stands are gone, the seats, the climbing littered aisles, most noticeably the overhanging friendly roof looming above it all—there's nothing up there where the smell of hot-dogs used to float around, where the shells of peanuts were cracked, where ice-cold pop was guzzled deliciously: there's nothing up there but a mass of rusted iron girders, naked arms pointing uselessly at the sky. The wreckers have done their work very thoroughly, very well indeed.

But strangely enough the right-field fence still remains almost over to centre field, and Rocky Nelson gives it one quick glance as he takes his place in the batter's box. Luke Hamlin's ready too, he gives his grimy, misshapen cap one last touch and toes the rubber. Then he lunges forward and throws a fast one on the outside corner to the left-handed batter that Rocky only watches streak by. A picture strike, waist-high, so that you wonder why Rocky wasn't waiting for that one, didn't paste it real good. But Rocky only shifts his chaw to the other side of his cheek, wiggling at the same time the lower half of his body (his feet, however, still in that half-turned-away stance that has puzzled baseball fans and writers alike for years, but works very well for him), takes another quick look out at Luke. Luke has finished tugging at his trouser belt, touches his cap and steps on the rubber again. He goes into his wind-up.

And the pitch? Surely not another fast one—Luke must know Rocky will be waiting for just such a surprise move as that. A change-up? The logical time to throw it, which is probably why he won't. Well then, how about a good, sharp-breaking curve cutting in close on the left-handed batter?

That's what it is, all right, breaking beautifully with a last-second twitch to it. Only trouble is, Rocky's spotted the pitch early, his bat comes around like it weighs no more than a tooth-pick in a lightning parallel arc to his body. The clean, sharp crack of swinging wood, real wood, meeting a baseball solidly head-on, is what we hear.

And as an announcer might say with just the right dramatic ring in his voice, there it goes, folks, bang down the right-field line but curving now a shade inside, still rising as it reaches the outfield grass, up, up, there it goes, ladies and gentlemen, a home run over the right-field fence with twenty or more feet to spare, still it goes on rising, rising, over the ghosts of Little Norway, over the marina and a hundred pleasure craft anchored at dockside, still rising as it moves out over the bay, heading for the Island, lost finally among all that green of water, blue of sky. . . .

Now more soberly we look around us, forced to realize at last that we are all alone in this great empty field of weed-high grass, with only the wreck of the gone-forever grandstand pointing up almost despairingly in the afternoon sunshine, no crowd or crowd-roar, only the endless rumble of traffic going by on Fleet Street.

And we know at last that we're witnessing one more little death among so many dyings—certainly life will go on, still beautiful and sometimes strange, but never in quite the same way as yet another boyhood fantasy goes under: after today not even the poet's wildest imaginings can make that world of baseball come alive again—brave, shining world of clean uniforms, of graceful, strategic manoeuvres—it's all gone, there's nothing left to do now but go on home, cheerfully if possible, this time without even a brightly coloured rain-check in the pocket, which found months later still promised baseball in another year. . . .

The Years
(1971)

THERE'S NO WAY OUT OF IT

There's no way out of it—
each leaf will sift down
slowly, grudgingly,
to the cold, bared ground,
grass won't push out
another blade of grass,
skies will do their best
to mirror the sun,
clouds will put their brightest,
their darkest faces on.

It will be all squirrels
and acorns (acorns anyway)
along the streets, maples red
and very proud for a week,
then humbled by the wind.
It will be so unlike death
that only pure fools and aging poets
will be taken in!

And all this happening
outside my window at this very moment
of a long, last September day;
with only one thing sure,
there's no way out of it.

YEAH, TIGERS

(For Bruce)

When our boy, Al Kaline, tagged that slider of Washburn's
in the third today, tagged it good, sent it sailing
high and deep in the Tigers' upper deck—

Wilf, I heard that yelp of yours
clear across this crummy town,
over TV bedlam, traffic, everything,

even if it only came out
as the slightest half-whisper
from your cancer-bugged throat.

259

OLD VETERANS, BATTERY DINNER

(For my father)

It's the end of the evening,
and though we were nodding in our chairs
as speaker after speaker droned on—

now we all rise up as one man,
and crossing arms over, join hands
with the comrade on either side of us,
to sing out above the piano, with feeling,
the words of Auld Lang Syne, not ashamed

if a tear should fall from our eye
as we think of our long-ago dead
and the newly dying, all those about us
who'll not stand with us singing here
this song or any other when a new year turns,
and old gunners sweat again up to the Line.

THE EYE

A thick mucous film
now covered the eyeball.

Out it comes or she'll die
our vet warned us.

Better have her destroyed,
someone else said.

Today she lives on
in our house,
Number One
one-eyed cat.

No trouble at all
with the good right eye
of our love.

THE PETITION

(For Bill)

The petition we're told
is addressed to the judge
who'll shortly sentence our friend
for drug trafficking.

We are being asked
to certify as to his standing
among our community of poets,
the idea being that the judge
may separate him from the usual drifters,
perhaps give him a lighter sentence,
six months instead of three years or four.

We are being asked
for very little, someone says,
it's no sweat at all to sign.
But still I can't feel
anything for this man
whom I've never met before
and know little of beyond the talk
that he uses drugs heavily. . . .

262

I look across this room
to where he sits quietly
while we discuss his case
(a mistake, I'm sure),
try to see what the face tells,
what the twitchy eyes reveal,
not what the beatnik sandals,
beads, the long hair, beard,
might seem to say.

Then I ask him a question
(as a judge might ask?)
about previous convictions,
and though his answer's favourable
I still can't believe what we do
in the end will have any chance
to cut his living hell in prison
to a bearable time,
repeat, can't feel the tie
of love or compassion for another,
can't move myself hard as I try
off my rock of isolation.

Someone says it again—
it's nothing, no trouble to sign.
Is that why all this crowd of poets
moves so eagerly now to scribble
on the required paper?
I really don't know,
but it seems this is all
we can do for our fellow-poet,
and I can't bring myself
to even this.

So the rest of the day
I'm ill-at-ease, this business
simply won't go away.
My mind keeps asking:
what's changed you,
how long has all this
been going on, how deep
is the cancer forked in,
how much of you
is still living flesh
beyond breathing and excretion,
eyes still opening at daylight?—

what separates you now
from the brutes,
from the unburied dead?

SUMMER FALLING

If I sit all day
watching closely,
I may see a whole rose fall
petal by petal
as the slight breeze stirs,
rocking each branch
just enough to end
any last reluctance:

summer falling
petal by petal
before my eyes.

264

THE GIRLS OF THE MORNING

By bus and by train
I'm pushed into morning;
but I twist in my seat,
close my eyes, imagine sleep.

But the girls of the morning
wait at every bus and train stop,
and I know it, how I know it!
So I find my eyes opening
as the doors are slid back
and crowds are loaded on
and stream off.

O the girls of the morning
are no girls dressed in mourning—
the skin of each shines
be it white, black or yellow
with the freshness of flower petals
newly opened, their hairdos
make them queens, flappers, innocents,
while their red lips hint passion,
eyes flash every tenderness.

O their perfumes fill the aisles
with the dreams of far islands,
their dresses shake the last
hint of sleep from our eyes
as the mini-skirts rise, dresses hug,
saris flow like water!

One and all proclaim
breasts waiting to be fondled,
legs waiting to be smoothed,
thighs waiting to be parted,
while posteriors on stairways
sway with that gentleness
badly needed in a world
of male rot and madness. . . .

O the girls of my morning
crying, shouting out love!

266

NOW WE TAKE YOU TO BIAFRA

They are dying, the commentator says,
from simple protein deficiency,
these children all eyes looking up
two each from their hospital beds.

It's morning now in Biafra,
a month from now this won't be news anymore.

No one will really care that a million starved to death—
what's a million people more or less in this world?

Their leaders claim they fight for independence,
so I suppose these children will continue to die
as long as there's a flag lifted up to wave
and young men willing to murder other men.

Count the scarecrow bodies by the thousand
as the camera takes a wide shot of the camp.

A month from now it won't even be news. . . .

During the next commercial I select
a cool tangerine from the refrigerator.

MAX

Max the adagio cat
leaping two ways at once
to paw a butterfly!

The orange-bright beauties
no longer so sure
of a safe one-way flight
across the garden. . . .

268

MEETING IN THE SUBWAY

I didn't ask this train to stall
in St. Andrew's Station (for fifteen minutes now),
certainly didn't ask
this young man and woman
to stand on the platform right in front
of the window where I happen to be sitting,
and argue back and forth.

He with his hands on his hips
and a look on his face that expresses a mixture
of patience and boredom. She more desperate-looking, almost
    ready
to burst into tears (or so I get the feeling),
if only to shift the harshness pain seems to bring
to her face, then behind the pleading eyes,
even under the entreating voice.

So it goes on—and not one word
mouthed by their lips can be heard—
what hatred, despair, even cruelty,
only theirs to really ever know;

leaving me, the unwitting onlooker,
unscheduled spectator, more than slightly glad
when at last the train jerks forward,
leaving them still behind on the platform,
with nothing resolved, or so it seems,
with still that casual hunch to his shoulders,
still that furrowed crease of pain between her eyes. . . .

BIG AL AT THE KICKING-HORSE

(For Al Purdy)

After nine or ten train wheels
had high-balled over me,
Big Al breathed hard from close by
"Kid, flex your stomach muscles real tight,
it's better to flip a few lousy box-cars
than end up having a hernia at your age."

LITTLE BOY LOST

I must have him, said the lake,
I want his pure white mouth sucked under
the weeds around my shore, I want his limbs
rocked in the gentle hammock of my waves.

No, he's mine, said the woods,
all mine to bury in a graveyard of fern,
all mine to tumble down a sudden slope,
all mine to numb with the frost of midnight.

No-one gets him but me
said the twisting, dusty road, no-one else
can take him from here to a better world,
though he may have to walk through an endless dark.

The lake, the woods, and that country road
all would have him that day—but his parents' arms,
outstretched and glad, took him back again—
so all three must be patient, wait another hour

when the next little boy comes along by the lake
with the woods overlooking, and at the top
a road that coughs in its midsummer heat—
all three must be patient and wait and wait. . . .

271

NOW THE MULBERRY'S FRUIT

Now the mulberry's fruit
sunned to purple of perfection,
juice itself to the touch,

presses down each branch
in a weight of abundance,
summer's warmest blessing.

All day long the birds,
magnet-drawn to pleasure,
flash their deep-stained beaks,

thrash about the clusters,
roused to frantic gorging,
roused to jubilation,

while the sun rides high
how that tree vibrates
to their myriad madness!

LA CROSSE

Box-la at Maple Leaf Gardens: the announcer
telling the small crowd at intermission:
"Tonight two full-blooded Indians from the Five Nations
   Reserve
are playing for Detroit Olympics. . . ."

In the second period one of them, Gaylord,
takes a cut at a Maple Leaf player
as though he knew all about tomahawks as well—

swings his lacrosse stick
much as those crafty Ottawas two centuries back,
staging their game on the English King's birthday
at Fort Michilimackinac—
                    all its gates wide open
for the holiday, the defenders drawn
to this game of a hundred savage men
knocking each others' brains out with gutted sticks—
then suddenly the ball innocently thrown
toward the fort, and the players swarming through the gates—

but these players carried tomahawks as well,
and with a blood-stopping shout la crosse was over
and a deadlier game, the massacre, began,
with British blood flowing on the ground to match
that already there from before. . . .

273

Well, Gaylord's no Ottawa
of Pontiac's, he's from a friendlier tribe,
but tonight shock-helmeted, shoulder-padded,
he's back at the wars, running end to end
in this giant arena with the roar that follows him
that of the white man who sits with his chips, his hot-dog,
watching the sticks flip that bullet-rubber ball
so expertly, the savage sweep of the goal shots—

and now a player knocked down, lying motionless,
with the crowd on their feet to a man, smelling blood....

A PRAYING MANTIS

A *preying* mantis
I can believe,
but a praying mantis—
never.

There simply isn't room
in this terror-guided world
for any creature large or small
with a name having such
a soft-bellied ring to it.

DEATH ON THE CONSTRUCTION SITE

Perhaps it was a sudden
unexpected gust of wind,
perhaps a fellow worker's carelessness—

anyway, twenty tons of steel came down *wham*,
and as it happens it was his day to die.

Nobody argues that his chest wasn't completely crushed,
nobody argues that he died without a single cry,
nobody argues that he died without any time for pain.

No time at all for the lowest vice-president of the corporation
to express a vote of thanks on behalf of the management,
no time certainly for the chairman of the board to press one
    drop of that blood,
one single piece of those bones into any part of the cornerstone,
no time as well for his comrades to ask that gleaming giant
    stretching up above them:
are you satisfied with this one death, or will you demand more
    before we finish?
No time at all for anything but call for the nearest stretcher,
cover up the body, carry it quickly away, don't forget to notify
    his wife,
no time to waste so let's get moving, boys, don't forget
we've still got a job to finish here. . . .

Only time to wipe so carefully away
any trace of his blood still remaining.

MORE INTERRUPTIONS LIKE THIS, PLEASE

A man needs steady hands
and all his wits about him
just to make his breakfast.

But when she arrives
like a sudden summer storm
fresh from the bath,
appears in the kitchen
exactly as God made her,

even posing, hands on hips,
inviting inspection—

no doubt about it
his toast is going to burn,
his coffee boil over,
while the cereal sits there,
mushy pulp in its bowl.

JEWELS

Who says nothing beautiful
ever happens in Toronto?

Just consider this—

Bobby Hackett coming suddenly
out of Whaley, Royce on Yonge Street,
holding in his hand a gleaming trumpet
which, catching the late rays
of the afternoon sun, makes jewels,
crown jewels flashing through my mind
long after he's waved for a taxi,
driven south into the soft auto haze. . . .

277

DON'T LAUGH

Don't laugh—for I promise you
ten, twenty years from now
you'll all be telling your grandchildren
with a kind of pride in your voice:

"I once saw Prime Minister Trudeau
walk along Bloor Street from Jane,
then stop in front of McLellan's jewelry store,
where he delivered a fine little speech,
signed autographs and was kissed
on the cheek by one middle-aged woman
who said she'd been a Liberal all her life—

and all on a cloudy cool Saturday morning
on the eighteenth of May
in the year of the Great Election of June '68."

TOP SECRET

TOP SECRET:
your building's coming down, Mrs. Brown,
probably some time next spring—
first the roof, then the upper floors,
all the way down to your own,
the high-ceilinged, shiny-floored main one.

Why do I call it yours?
Who really but me has any good claim to it
beside yourself—and mine so very slender
beside your own. I would guess you spent
a quarter of your life on your knees,
first scrubbing the surface dirt from that stubborn floor
with cleaner so ammonia-strong
I used to choke just on one small whiff of it,
then rubbing the paste-wax in till the sweat
streamed down your face, then worked on your glasses,
so you had to stop, fog-bound, till you'd wiped them clear. . . .

You gave your life for that floor, Mrs. Brown,
and it never properly deserved one day of your toil.
Its smug face polished up like glass
only laughed back at you from your very first meeting
right through to that last aching time,
when, with head turning circles, stomach sick,
you left, never to return. . . .

Your building's coming down, Mrs. Brown,
and you should be buried under it
And your grave plainly marked. But cleaning ladies are
    expendable,
a dime a dozen, and sentiment, they all tell me,
is a major weakness, Mrs. Brown.

GRIGIO

Forgive me, Old Grey One,
for thinking that the water
on our kitchen floor came
from your ancient bladder,
instead, as it turned out,
from your tongue which now
won't stay in or stop drooling.

Forgive me, Grigio,
most stately of cats,
and don't forget you're always
most welcome in this house.

Just let us know
whenever you want in.

SMALL HOUSE IN A SMALL TOWN

If the mud-swallows nested in your eaves
it was said you had bed-bugs for sure.

Mice made it hard to go to sleep
with the footraces up and down the walls.

Lizards scatter-scuttled like crazy
when a light shone down the earthen cellar stairs.

And one Christmas Eve the roof blew off
and we almost froze to death before morning.

A LETTER TO BIAFRA

I once sent a letter to Biafra
but received no reply.

I've often wondered
if it ever got there,

and if it did,
was there anyone still alive
to answer it.

DEATH CHANT FOR MR. JOHNSON'S AMERICA

America
you seem to be dying
America
moving across the forty-ninth parallel each day a stronger,
more death-laden stench;
wafting inshore from off the Great Lakes the same unmistakable stink, so unlike the usual putrefaction of these waters

America
the cracks are beginning to show
America
I knew you were marching to doom the night a young American told me: "There at Buffalo I saw our flag flying, then fifty yards farther on your Maple Leaf, and I thought: thank God I'll never have to cross that line going back again."
America
even your best friends of yesterday are now proud to be your enemies
America
that time is past when the sight of your Stars and Stripes flying at the masthead of your ships can calm "the natives"; that time too is over when a detachment of Marines on landing can still restore law and order along with a continuation of the prescribed vested interests
America
there will be no more San Juan Hills, no more Remember the Maines, no more sad empires of United Fruit,

America
your time is running out fast
America
you haven't changed at all since you sent your New York State
farm boys across the Niagara to conquer us once and for
all, since you printed your handbills promising French-
Canadians sweet liberation from their oppressors, since you
looked the other way as Fenians played toy soldiers across
our border

America
you're sitting on your own rumbling volcano
America
only you could create a New York where a new breed of white
rats chase slum children through rotting rooms, biting into
infant flesh with much the same relish that some tailor's
dummy shows at the exact same moment downtown as he
takes his first mouthful of ten-dollar steak while beaming
across at his equally over-dressed partners also pressing her
teeth into the meat course,
only you could create squads of drunks lying in doorways,
addicts readying fixes in dirty washroom heavens, only you
could build these terrifying buildings reaching up through
the dirt, noise and smog-death for a breath of clean air
somewhere at the thousand-foot level,
only you could fashion East River mountains of used cars,
graveyards of King Auto more mysterious than elephant
burial grounds, only you could spawn the greed and corruption of a Wall Street with its ticker-tape, fortune-cookie
dreams, its short-sell nightmares,
only you could conceive this monster, and only you will be the
one to destroy it pier by pier, block by block, citizen by
citizen,

America
you seem bent on self-destruction
America
today you are Ginsberg's nightmare brought up-to-date, today
you would sicken Hart Crane, make him puke on his Brook-
lyn Bridge, today you're fast becoming Jeffers' perishing
republic all set to vanish in one final blast with the rest of a
despairing world
America
you seem bent on taking that world along with you just for the
ride

America
phoney as a Hollywood main street, laughable as Rockefeller
with his ten-cent pieces, vulgar as a Las Vegas nightclub,
brave as your airmen machine-gunning river-front refugees
in broad daylight of Dresden's holocaust
America
you have learned from everyone's history but your own
America
all the Kennedys left alive cannot help you now

America
I've learned how you operate, I know how votes are controlled,
who has his coat pockets stuffed with bribes, who finds himself asked to be Assistant Secretary of this or that, who is
tossed out finally with nothing left but bitterness eating at
his heart,

America
you kept Pound locked up all those years—he had you pegged
—Usura; he had you dead to rights, betrayers of Jefferson,
he had you figured out good so you left him caged and
cooking in the sun at Pisa to drive him mad—but he put the
record straight about Roosevelt; you hoped to bury him forever in St. Elizabeth's, but instead he walks a free (though
broken) man now, his vision haunting you with its signa-
ture of doom

America
was promises nobody has kept or even intended keeping
America
how do you turn quiet, home-loving men in five short years
into hate-fired Black Muslim avengers who write, scream
out to their brothers: break doors, smash windows at night
or anytime, bust in every store-front, drag out all you can
carry, set fire, kill or maim Whitey, pump holes into every
dirty cop or get him good with a brick or your own two
hands

America
give it all back to the Indians if they can stand all the smell
and the flies around the corpse
America
how easily your myths tarnish, how expendable your heroes,
how quickly, how easily you swallow good people into your
patented garbage disposal, grinding them down into nice
little pieces to be carted away to the dump with almost the
same care accorded the ashes of dead Japanese soldiers (but
nonetheless garbage, waste products of your restless, unsatisfied ambition hanging like a giant cancer cloud, a plague
of slowly spreading death over the world)

285

America
you have been tested and found wanting
America
the world has watched you in Vietnam and even its terror-hardened stomach has been turned, you have all but buried yourself in your own Coca-Cola, beer-can litter, your bar-to-bar Saigon filth aped so well by the small men you came to save but instead have corrupted forever;

after your crazy "weed-killer" squadrons have bared all the trees, after your Incinderjell has roasted all the available corpses, then perhaps we'll see at last every barbed-wire death-camp, count every tin-can house left standing, see how much rice still grows

after the last plane has been shot down out of the sky we'll see at last who still owns all the graft concessions, who hands out the government payoffs, opens unnumbered Swiss bank accounts daily

but until then we're forced to watch as your Marines advance, as the underground bunkers are cooked out one by one, as the aircraft let go their terror bombs still hoping these latest villages hold a few more VC than the ones raided yesterday

the whole world watches, wonders how it will end, while you continue to entwine yourself more and more in the dragon coils of your own premeditated meddling

America
there is nothing really left to do but die with a certain gracefulness
really nothing left to do
America
in the name of God whom you never trusted, e pluribus unum

February, 1968

286

America
tonight fiery candles of the black man's mass burn crimson in
    the skies of Washington, Chicago, tributes from the ghettos
    to your Gandhi struck down cowardly by bullets of hate,
the Gun used again to work out history, the Gun in the hands
    of the lawless once again making jungles of your streets,
    mockery of your laws,
the Gun that gave you birth, that burned on its red-hot gun-
    barrel flesh of brother turned savagely against brother
once again supreme
America

so bring out the machine-guns, unsling the shot-guns, line up
    the sights from the armoured-car,
shoot to kill, shoot to kill, shoot to kill
kill kill kill
America

April 5, 1968

287

THE HIPPIES AT NATHAN PHILLIPS SQUARE

Completely unaware
and I'm sure not caring
that the Superintendent of Sanitary Sewers
together with his colleague
the Assistant Director of Garbage Disposal
watched them from the solid ninth tier
of New City Hall's flashing windows,

the young, bearded, unkempt boy
camped out below on the Square,
waved a greeting from his sleeping-bag
to the long-haired blonde
with bare toes showing in her sloppy joes,

and helped her
as she wiggled in beside him,
was then last seen as his hand reached out
and zippered up the bag. . . .

In the bright morning sunlight
that sleeping-bag was seen
first to shake, then to roll,
indeed was the most moving thing
in all of Nathan Phillips Square.

At that point the Superintendent
of Sanitary Sewers
suddenly remembered he'd been
on the way to the washroom all the time,
while the Assistant Director
of Garbage Disposal
suddenly recalled he was two minutes late
for his appointment with the mayor. . . .

THE CONFRONTATION

While it certainly burned him having to pay $2.50 for an Expo passport just to exercise his rights of freedom of speech—

it seemd a bargain as the President of the Home of the Brave finally loomed into view, surrounded it seemed by at least a hundred plainclothes men, and even more so as the President passed close to him and he shouted out loud as his poet's hatred could stir within him, "BLOODY BUTCHER!"

But he might have known it wouldn't be quite that easy— you couldn't begin to throw off a slow century of tradition with a moment's inflamed utterance; while a good upbringing was bound to intrude no matter how hard you fought against it—

so that he found himself, as he was led away (not by two Secret Service but by ordinary québécois flics!), forced to make a concession after all, though it hurt him deeply, and though no-one could possibly hear him above the commotion as he shouted out again, "BLOODY BUTCHER—*sir*!"

THE CRITIC

Soul, when next you see
this Thing coming toward you,
simply shut your mouth tight
and move out as fast
as your fat calves will carry you.

For his prying eyes dig
into the darkest corners,
his great ears pick up
all sounds and distort them
like disgruntled tuning-forks.

He is worse than Death
and he is everywhere.

PEACE DEMONSTRATION

The six thin girls
of the Viet Cong who steal
into the Marine camp, calmly shoot
four men to death,
then escape in the dark,
know what they're doing and why.

The young Yankee paratrooper
on the night patrol looking for VC
also knows: kill the enemy impersonally,
with the least use of ammunition.

His President in the White House
hasn't any doubts,
or if he has hides them very well
in his news conferences.

That aging revolutionary in Hanoi
can't afford to waver:
a lifetime's sacrifice dearly bought
flashes always before his eyes.

So it is left for these,
our restless, unfulfilled youth
of the sit-ins, peace marches,
to carry the burden of guilt
for all of us: spelling it out
on their crude, homemade signs,
hammering it home as the police
move in to drag them,
night-stick them into waiting paddy-waggons:

these, the worst scarred,
the most bewildered,
the truly worse than dead.

FIVE NIGHTHAWKS

Five nighthawks down a late August sky
like all things earthly given wings to fly,
soared, checked, dived, hung as though suspended
between night unborn and a day not yet ended.

292

THE PROBLEM

How to share the aching feet
of the already limping
deliverer of handbills.

REMEMBRANCES

Her cat likes to hide her socks,
but likes even more to lie
in a mound of her pyjamas or chew
a pair of her panties; in short, almost anything
reminding it of her, her woman's odour,
the warmth of her body still lingering
in the least thing she's worn.

While her man has carefully hidden
an old girdle, a discarded pair of stockings,
a sun-suit she never liked and wore only once,
saving them just in case there comes a time
when she'll finally tire of him and shed him
as coolly and completely as when she steps
from her clothing at the end of the day.

Then he'll reach to the back of a drawer,
bring her somehow back to him again,
breathing deep scents clinging still to silk and cotton.

ALMOST LAST VISIT TO AN OLD TOWN

Your holiday's been a bust—
not one comfortable chair
among all the antiques in the rented apartment,
and moth-ball smell to boot!

You say: before I'd live here again
I'd die first: the kind of talk
I try to pass off lightly
but somehow can't.
Then afternoon sun catching in its stride
each window down the street
gives me a little hope.

This town that outlived
and lived down Leacock surely will forgive
our own irreverences. And remember,
high on the hillside, hard by the water-tower,
those were happy years. When you could laugh
at winter floodings, summer dryness,
cicadas' bedlam shriek
choked finally by snow-drifts.
Or so it seemed when time and its four seasons
melded, blessed you all at once!

294

THE CAGE

I haven't seen you on the main floor
for almost a month, she tells me,
they seem to keep your animals
well caged down there. . . .

We both smile at her joke (an old one),
knowing well the real animals, the true monsters
of this world are never caged up,
or even locked up for a moment,

but are left free to do their killing,
often without the slightest trace of a mark
on a thousand, ten thousand victims,
are called "sir" in clubs,
will cause good men to jump as on a string
when their name is announced, when the telephone rings.

And these animals live in large houses on very quiet streets,
have obedient, loving wives who endure every loneliness, every
    pain,
and often, just to show the weakness in the breed,
have at least one untamed, very beautiful daughter.

CLOSE TO HOME

Our big cat watches
an almost tolerant look in the eyes,

as our six-weeks-old kitten
claws at his tail or charges headlong
at the giant across from him,

the little one knowing very well by now
that he'll be thrown easily down,
but still coming back again and again for more. . . .

The Yankee the Viet Cong
at war each night
on the carpeted battleground
of our living-room.

FIRST SNOWFLAKE

The first snowflake always has
the longest, loneliest journey.

A million comrades watch
on a night of shivers
as it casts off from Mother Cloud,
then flutters, slips and slides away,
all very much down.

When, after several eternities,
the watchers see their brother finally touch
some distant part of earth,
it's as if a giant string were pulled
with dark turned inside out,
and all white now, all shine,
and falling falling falling.

THE GREAT WHITE LOCUSTS

As my Moroccan friend,
Maurice, might say:

Allah be merciful
and save us all

from the Great White Locusts of Christmas!

TWO TAUNTING CROWS

Two taunting crows
flapped over us
as the first snow fell.

"Freeze, dead heads,
freeze,"

they croaked rightly.

A KIND OF *VOYEUR*

My oldest cat's
a *voyeur* like his master,
not the peep-hole variety
but the wide window-gazer kind,
in which everything passing by
is worth at least a second look,
cars, children, dogs of course, other cats,
while anything with birds has him tail-twitching,
nervously come alive.

Most of all he seems to treasure
the sudden action, simple tragedy,
suddenly stirring on the window's other side,
which he can watch almost as one involved,
really living it through, at the same time be safe
from all hurt or difficult decision,
like looking out from a part of the world
to another part close by:
can tremble with rage or passion,
lust for the sight of blood
without lifting a paw,
without taking a claw.

FOOL'S DAY

Even with all
his jester's bells and flowers
he won't impress many.

This city's full up,
brimming over with fools.
So one more who's well publicized,
even dressed for the part,

can't expect to cause the slightest stir
today or any other day
in Nathan Phillips Square.

300

MOURNING DOVE

1

Mourning dove
morning dove

who but you
would stay so long

with only one
sad song?

2

I don't need a mourning dove
hugging my house
half the night and day,
inviting me to join
in his miniature fog-horn
half-moans of sorrow.

I have my own dark times,
but I try to keep my sorrows
carefully to myself,

so that with the years
they've now become
a guarded, precious treasure.

FIRST REPORT TO THE MILITARY GOVERNOR

"In the City of Toronto itself
only one incident, and even that
hardly worthy of record.

One of our tanks
in circling their city-hall square,
brushed against a large piece of sculpture
(purchased, they tell me,
from an Englishman named Moore);

at which their mayor
who had witnessed the accident,
stormed from his council chamber
shaking both fists at our troops,

who, not sharing his concern,
seized him and strung him up
(by the golden chain of office
he happened to be wearing)
on that same odd-shaped casting,
where I'm told he swung very slowly
like a pendulum keeping
not very accurate time—

whose body, however,
I'm very proud to report,
wasn't hung by the heels
like that sad man Il Duce,

which shows if nothing else
the good sense and moderation
of our Glorious Revolution
of November 31st."

WAITING FOR THE RAIN TO END

Up on front porches, beneath roofs that overhang,
men are starting the morning out by watching
rain falling by them, down and down and down.

Waiting patiently for the end of this whim of the elements
so they can finish the bricks that become a wall,
lay sewer-pipes sweatingly, rip up tired roadways,
all the necessary businesses no-one ever thinks of.

All over this city so many eyes are looking up
at the falling rain, wishing, quietly urging it over,
that I predict by ten the sun will have to burst through
if only for the heavens to keep its peace with man.

303

MAN WITH CLUBFOOT

When he was very young
and his first black boot
with its four-inch rise
had been fitted on,

he remembered his mother
smiling brightly as she said:
some day very soon
you'll go out for a walk
and you won't feel you have it on. . . .

But tonight,
fifty-odd years later,
as he climbs these stairs
the weight of that foot
feels almost unbearable,
and his mother no longer
still alive to ask
how much longer to wait
for that promised day.

THE HOUSE

Up above
broadloom's deep

walls gleam
hi-fi booms.

Underneath
drains bulge

garbage festers
rats swarm.

NOT REALLY FOR PUBLICATION

My kidneys weakening,
my eyes getting worse—
enough to make any man
start rhyming his verse!

305

IT'S NOT THAT EASY

We try to look cheerful, to smile,
as we go around the office shaking hands,
wishing one another Happy New Year;

but it's not quite that easy
with over thirty-two hours
of loneliness, betrayal, loss,
still left in the old one.

306

FORECAST

Although my best nightmare
is easily violent highway death—
me leaving the centre line
to pass the slowpoke ahead,
then not spotting the oncoming car
moving like a rocket till the last
stabbing terror of his headlights—

and although I sense my luck
has certainly run out by now
at crosswalks and most street-corners—

I now forecast my almost certain death
on a warm day like this, the heat haze
pressing iron-heavy down in the streets,
with no real sun willing to shine through,

both lungs of mine refusing at long last
to breathe another single choking breath
of blue-coated, evil-swirling exhaust smoke.

CHEMNITZ ATTACK, FEBRUARY 14/15, 1945

(An RCAF aircrew veteran speaks)

To the credit of the Limeys
this time at briefing
they didn't feed their crews
the same Dresden BS,
i.e., "you are attacking
a Gestapo headquarters,"
or "a vital ammunitions works,"
or "a large poison-gas factory. . . ."

Instead the briefing officers
of 3 Group laid it
squarely on the line:
"We are going to finish off
any refugees who may have escaped
last night's Dresden attack. . . ."

But of course we Canadians
got the same crap again
we'd had the night before:
"Tonight your target is Chemnitz,
a large manufacturing centre
with an important rail junction
and numerous repair-shops. . . ."

So our crew went out
in "V" for "Victory"
on its first nervous op
against the enemy,
with the Met boys all wrong
and the clouds ten-tenths,
so we bombed very wide
on sky-markers, which I guess

is what helped save Chemnitz
and fifty thousand more
of its people from death
and being piled up, stacked cordwood,
waiting to be burned
in the city squares. . . .

But the evil part is—
none of this known
until thirty years after,
leaving me more disillusioned,
more suspicious than ever
of words mouthed or written
by men of goodwill,
of incorruptible minds,

knowing they are men
and no-one is guiltless,
no-one ever free
of the blood of innocents.

DEMOLITION IN AUGUST

*(Demolition site, Bank of Toronto building, King and Bay
Streets, Toronto, August 1966. The three stone faces affixed to
the north wall speak out for the last time as the wall is being
torn down around them)*

TIMOTHY: Good gentlemen,
how else would you want me to say it?
What a shoddy ending—
demolition by Greenspan!

BENJAMIN: We, the ears, noses, eyes
of all the Gooderhams!

NICHOLAS: These columns below,
these façades above us,
the solid pride
of a kinder generation!

TIMOTHY: A proud, God-fearing,
Empire-loving generation.

BENJAMIN: Generation without benefit
of the Pill or the Bomb.

NICHOLAS: When a man knew his place
and stayed within it,
when women were content in the home....

TIMOTHY: Remember how this marble high-sparkled
the year these walls began to rise?

NICHOLAS: Nothing but the smoothest
most expensive Carrara-cut
shipped direct from Italy.

BENJAMIN: It was said the stone
would turn a gentle pink
after three years' weathering,
but no-one quite reckoned
on the filth of this city.

TIMOTHY: A fog of death
choking inch by inch
the life from each piece of stone.

NICHOLAS: The evils of today
at work even then—
only no-one noticed
or if they did, said nothing.

TIMOTHY: But still you must admit
we've seen enough up here
to last any lifetime.

BENJAMIN: Wars and celebrations
of peace, then more wars,
a too-familiar cycle!

NICHOLAS: Success and bold ruin,
every pinnacle, every depth.

TIMOTHY: Remember 1914?
Thick crowds through the summer nights,
endless parades, mass recruiting,
a world gone mad or worse.

BENJAMIN: And 1918—
that first false Armistice.
The birth if you will
of a new hysteria.

NICHOLAS: Then at last
the return of the heroes—
one in ten less
than those who marched away.

BENJAMIN: The discreet betrayal
of all they'd fought for
visible and growing
in the slightly madhouse
years racing by.

TIMOTHY: Bay Street the grubby
gambling tout of the nation,
City Hall a sewer
to corruption's cesspools.

BENJAMIN: The Crash almost seemed
at first sight a blessing—
stern chance for a fresh
beginning of the heart.

NICHOLAS: But blight had been planted
too deeply in the soul,
cancer leaped through living tissue.

TIMOTHY: We seemed to almost welcome
this darkness of the soul,
content to lick our own vomit.

NICHOLAS: Waiting for a miracle,
deliverance at the hands
of a new Messiah.

BENJAMIN: So forgetful that we
and we alone
stamp the shape of our destiny.

TIMOTHY: When at last that fear
seemed slowly to be lifting,
we found ourselves menaced
by an even darker terror—
the Nazi war machine!

BENJAMIN: Remember the day
our proud 48th paraded,
how heads were held high
to the pipes' skirling!

NICHOLAS: But only a few
loud cheers from the crowd,
even bagpipes
couldn't brace divided hearts.

TIMOTHY: The months of hell ahead
cunningly shown about town
on recruiting posters
as a free world tour,
all expenses paid.

BENJAMIN: Airmen scarcely ready to shave,
soldiers mere boys out of school,
sailors born two thousand miles
from any ocean.

NICHOLAS: But each man as eager
as their fathers before them
to prove up their manhood
for the nation to see,
as if this were all
there was left to do anyway. ...

BENJAMIN: But we linger, gentlemen,
much too long in the past—
don't forget *we* may be
museum pieces by tomorrow!

TIMOTHY: Or worse, unless someone
has room for three unshaved
rather solemn-faced ancients!

BENJAMIN: No respect alive today
for the old or antiquated.
Big Ben up the street there
may very soon suffer
the same odious lynching.

NICHOLAS: This city caught up
in the maddest of scrambles
to turn all its streets
into twenty-storey mausoleums.

TIMOTHY: The Jet Age saluted
to the relentless rhythms
of the wrecking-ball!

BENJAMIN: When even the cow gates
of Osgoode are threatened
by a new breed of vandals.

NICHOLAS: Come now, gentlemen,
let's not find ourselves
bowing out ungracefully.

TIMOTHY: Agreed; it well may be
that's all we have left now,
a certain dignity.

BENJAMIN: A dubious legacy
we leave behind
for these strangers to ponder.

NICHOLAS: So be quiet, gentlemen,
try to spend these last hours
in peaceful contemplation.

BENJAMIN: At least we'll be spared
the unknown horrors of a time
so unlike any other.

TIMOTHY: But still miss the joys—
shall we leave it at that,
good gentlemen?

315

PORTRAIT OF THE ARTIST AS A YOUNG MAN WELL-ROLLED IN MONTREAL

(For Ron and Lorna, who will remember)

Will there ever come a morning,
when, without knowing it,
someone will shift one lid back
to see by the naked eyeball
if you're still alive, decide that you are,
then gently shake you awake?

Next come your eyes opening on other eyes
looking down on you, your head sending signals
of pain now through all your body;
head that appears, as you slowly raise yourself,
to have rested all night on the curved metal pillow
of a switchbox cover in the dark oil-smell
of a garage, one you note hazily
with expensive cars parked.

Then, as you stand on your feet,
kind hands brush the dust from your suit;
you make a quick reflex of looking at your watch
but it's not there to give you even a clue,
and then you find your wallet's gone,
money, papers, everything.

And will you ever find yourself muttering
as you stand there, still only half in the world,
"I'm ashamed, I'm so ashamed of all this,"
and take the two dollars someone hands you for cab fare,
still saying the same words over, "I'm so ashamed..."?

And will you be even more ashamed
not to know what those words really mean anymore?

FOR IKUKO FROM THE TWO OF US

When you entered this house
I'm sure the front door shook,
while you stayed with us
all four walls glowed.

Now you are gone
it seems our hearth-stone
has no wish to laugh
until your return.

OLD LAKE LIGHT, HANLAN'S POINT

(For Ted Enslin)

Not content with the poem
which may lie with the bones
of the strangely murdered
first keeper of this light
(said buried near his place of work),

you pry back the unused door
to the narrow stairway,
then brushing back cobwebs
begin to climb
the wooden stairs spiralling,

with me following one
or two steps close behind
your woodsman's boots,
raising years-quiet dust
(quiet, dull Canadian
of dour Toronto
behind the restless
probing New Englander),

knowing very well
that nothing much lies
at the light's weathered top
but the choppy lake ahead,
calm saucer of the reservoir
if we choose to turn around.

But sensing somehow
that even this
you'll manage to transform
into something immediate,
something almost new,
worth a hundred times and more
this circling climb.

319

FOR BAY STREET CHARLIE

"Bay Street's my life, my home."

Words well oiled
by a few stiff drinks
that night on the *Cayuga's*
noisy moonlight cruise.

And now I've started on you
let's finish it—for who's to say
how wild my nightmare of you
really is?
        That one where,
like a giant stuck toad,
you lie right in the middle
of King and Bay's intersection
while traffic mounts bedlam around you,
and even four pairs of arms
can't seem to budge you at all—

can't budge
a thousand Steak 'n Burger dinners,
a thousand Pickwick Tavern pints
(three hundred twenty seven pounds
your triple soles refuse to carry
another inch along the pavement).

I call it a nightmare—
but there's also the dread of you going
at a time when we can't afford to lose
even one familiar face, one more friendly hand
(not at least in this dead-about-the-heart locality).

So now that I've said this much
you might as well hear the rest—
the day you exit more than one of us will feel
our doom more certain, will sense the street
in its relentless way more surely closing in.

Street that somehow, Charlie,
you've helped to make us love.

321

Change-Up
(1974)

YORKVILLE AVENUE

Flies clinging to the table-cloth
even with the last crumb gone.

Such young, age-whitened faces!

Waiting through the hours
for food, dope, money,

love.

IN A MOMENT OF ANGER

(Pierre Laporte assassinated)

The first murder's
the most difficult,
the one that separates
the men from the boys.

Now that it's done
the rest will be easier,
almost routine,

and you and your kind
can be almost assured
of a place in history
with all other assassins.

OTTAWA FOR ME

Ottawa for me, George Johnston,
lies at the bottom of your street,
lies where Third Avenue ends
and the canal begins—
canal of green-drowsing water
into which the leaves
of autumn were dropping
one slow leaf at a time,
with each doomed one wandering down
bringing winter closer, surer in. . . .

Ottawa for me
is no longer the Château,
the Parliament Buildings,
Confederation Square,
for in some strange way
it's become this canal
sleeping softly under the trees
(I wonder now if Lampman came here,
ever once thought of ending it all
looking down into this still, still water,
then shrugging his shoulders walked back
to Slater Street, to life again. . . ?)

And perhaps the canal only sleeps
dreaming of the day both sides
of her mighty river will become as one,
waiting with that beautiful patience
we both felt yesterday I'm sure,
looking out across this placid water
when the early autumn leaves were falling
one eternity at a time, George,
one eternity at a time.

TRACKS IN THE SNOW

Others have been here ahead of me,
but I still choose my own way through the snow;
hoping, if my tracks are big and straight enough,
someone may follow in mine.

SNOWPLOUGH

All day long a snowplough snorts
up and down the street,
shaking the houses,
rattling these bookshelves.

A cat yawns.
Our lives remain unmoved.

326

THE TOUCH

Starts toward me unsteadily
across the wind-whipped subway platform.

Lays a hand softly on my shoulder,
looks at me with the life
all but burned out from his eyes.

"I'm a North American Indian,
I got no place to stay tonight,
have a few cents to spare?"

I place a dollar bill
almost too quickly in his hand.
"Happy New Year," I say
when no other words will come.

Then walk away as he starts to cry
a little like a child.

SHIPWRECKED

He sits on a bench
in the nine AM chill,
but his hands aren't shaking
from the cold.

He can't stop them,
they've left his body,
they belong to someone else.

He's a young man, too,
his face hardly aged.

The policeman who's found him
now uses his walkie-talkie
to call a patrol car

that will soon whisk him away
to wherever, whatever
drunks are thrown into.

In the full-page ads,
on TV
or even in the subway,

today's smart drinkers are shown
as handsome, well dressed,
always surrounded by many
young and beautiful women
glasses held just so:

the bastards never show them
crowded into drunk-tanks
hardly able to breathe,
still retching a little,
or clawing at the walls
in an effort to escape
the oncoming slimy
crawling, multiplying beetles.

PICTURES FROM A LONG-LOST WORLD: 1912

The young officers of cavalry
fresh from Sofia sit stiff-backed on horses
as they shout across the now-silent battlefield.

It has been a most glorious victory.
Another Turkish fort captured
with a loss of only fifty soldiers.

Dead comrades lie at their horses' feet.
They lie singly or piled together.
If there's time they'll be buried,
if not buzzards will strip them clean.

In this year of rapid advances
nothing is certain.

THE END OF SUMMER

Frenzied whine
of cicada's bandsaw
is silent now.

The only wood left uncut
that branch he's fastened to.

THE SIGN

NO BATHING WEEKENDS
SWIMMING WEEKENDS THROUGH SEPTEMBER
WEATHER PERMITTING

But unfortunately the sandpipers
never get far enough up the beach
to read these instructions,

and so go about
their business of breaking
the law so naturally,
so easily, so beautifully,

you could say it's almost a crime
to have to watch them.

FIRST HOLIDAY MORNING

Easily morning's earliest,
most beautiful, laziest thought—

you lying beside me
far away in sleep,
while all through this city
alarum-clocks are piercing brains,
breakfasts are being gobbled,
sleepy faces smear on lipsticks, creams,
blades nick too deeply into skins,

then suddenly car exhausts roar,
buses pack in bodies to spew them
underground into subway trains
for short, flashing mole-deep rides
to offices still asleep themselves,
to streets still yawning in the weekend dust. . . .

There the thought mercifully ends—
returns to you
resting easily beside me,
then leaves me again as I
try to hunt you out,
catch up to you,

with any luck walk beside you
in some strange country you are almost entering now.

331

FEBRUARY WIND

The wind that hollows my cheeks
impresses me only. That half-moon shrouded
by a yellow mist points up a cat
who starts to cross my path,
then thinks better of it.

I seem to be the only one walking out
in my neighbourhood tonight, unless I count
that cat still lurking somewhere, and one boy
alone on the unlighted hockey cushion—
some young Frank Mahovlich making it the hard way—
the puck his stick slap-shoots
rattling the end boards, goal, goal, goal!

I go on down the street. Let the wind take me,
do with me what it will. One gust may come along
to blow me up through the trees, then higher, higher,
until I touch down frostily on the moon.

THIS ROSE

This rose asks nothing,
neither to be bought,
nor ever loved
or even admired.

It wishes only to bud,
then to bloom
for two short weeks
in the sun.

Then it is quite resigned
to being torn apart
petal by petal
and scattered down the wind,

to blind with dust
then with earth,
to feel the damp ground's
shivering final kiss.

333

HOLDING HANDS IN THE LIBRARY

Sitting across from each other,
long-haired girl
long-haired boy.

Books spread open on the table
but they aren't being looked at any more.

She was writing in her notebook
but that was ten minutes ago.

Now they hold hands across the table,
stroke palms, touch fingers
across that wooden surface,
even talk in low whispers.

They're in love,
you can see that easily enough;
how wonderful
that look on their faces!

What they're learning now
no textbook could ever teach them,

what they know at this moment
no footnote could ever reveal.

Every last book in this library
feels how very dead it is.

334

BACK LANE

Back lane leading south off the Avenue,
lane leading south and everywhere and nowhere, lane of
childhood and manhood, lane of the junk collector, rapist,
molester, young lovers, playing children, drunks and old men,
lane of early morning fronting on sunken back porches,
sagging walls, broken windows, with scrawny cats on those
same broken windows; no green anywhere, what little grass
choked under gravel and concrete, the few remaining trees too
sick, too tired to reach straight up toward the sun, their
branches broken, twisted semaphores,
lane of this year's throw-outs, of last year's discards—yel-
lowed newspapers heavy with the filth and death of all our
hopes, an abandoned toilet-seat holding once what curve of
beauty, the ripped-open guts of sofas on which how many lies
were woven, how many dream-castles shaped; smashed bottles
heavy still with the fingerprints of what unknown agonies,
what blood-stained despairs,
lane of mysterious oil smells, cooking smells, urine smells,
turd smells, all baked and kneaded by the sun, the rain into
earth and pavement, now all hanging in the air, suspended
there as if forever,
lane suddenly ending on this half-lit side-street, lane now
suddenly come alive, made human again by the smile of the
young Chinese girl who arrives from nowhere and sings out to
me: "Hey, mister, hey, mister," whose short legs, black head go
as quickly as they came, leaving spring air sifting through this
lane somehow warmer, more gentle, more life-giving in its
touch!

THIRTEEN DAYS OF DEATH

(Cuban missile crisis, October 1962)

There came that afternoon
when I helped a middle-aged couple
(who'd driven in that morning from Beamsville)
carry their six gold bars from our vault
to their car waiting in a parking-lot.
Dutch-born, the woman said the Nazis
had stolen all their money the last time,
but this time the bloody Russians
wouldn't get one cent of theirs....

That was the very same week
my wife and I seriously debated
where we'd hide our excrement
if forced to live down in the cellar
for a week or so.
We finally agreed: to hell with it,
waited upstairs for the bombs to whistle over.

Waiting for death, though,
somehow subtly marked us,
we'd never be quite the same again.
Our radio blared,
the television confused us more than ever.

336

Then we watched smiling President Kennedy
announce with those tired crinkly eyes
still working TV magic,
that the Russians were removing their missiles,
were going home like good little boys from Cuba.
No cheers, only numbness.
After all, hadn't *we* been the ultimate stakes
in this greatest of draw-poker games?

Yes, we could breathe easily again,
and because we only wanted to forget
how teeter-totter close we'd come
to total oblivion I'm afraid
we forgot much too fast. . . .

Then it was only years later
we learned their sweet-smiling Kennedy had had
two safer, more reasonable choices,
but characteristically decided "Damn the experts,"
bluffed it out to his last show-down hand
with big-dealer Krushchev:
using us (to repeat) as the little pile
of coloured chips in the pot,
and only one ending for the game—
life or death. . . .

337

QUEEN ANNE'S LACE

It's a kind of flower
that if you didn't know it
you'd pass by the rest of your life.

But once it's been pointed out
you'll look for it always,
even in places
where you know it can't possibly be.

You'll never tire
of bending over to examine,
of marvelling at this
shyest filigree of wonder
born among grasses.

You'll imagine poems
as brief, as spare,
so natural with themselves
as to take your breath away.

338

WRECKERS' PROGRESS

(For Lia)

Turning the now all-too-familiar corner
I note the wreckers have our old home-away-from-home
chopped off very neatly to the second floor,
our floor, seem to pose there with crowbars and shovels
as if waiting for cameras to flash.

Just think, roughly about where they're all standing now,
you once came through a door cunning as a cobra
and threw your arms around me as I sat
in the boss' chair—while the whole office roared!

OLD MILL BY FLOODLIGHT

I'm sure old man Fisher
would flip in his grave tonight
if he could use my eyes, stare acros this valley
to where his mill stands in silhouette,
three upper windows gaping squares of black
with their top sills nowhere as the ruin ends in air:

taking for a roof (or so it seems from here)
some part of the gleaming length of the subway bridge—
and here is the marvel—across which at this very moment
twelve shining cars of a train seem to ride
or float or slide or glide—or anything you want them to. . . .

NOW THAT APRIL'S HERE

He smiling, eager
curly-headed Adam,

she dark-haired
temptress Eve,

tongue-and-ear kissing
on the subway platform
(what's coming next?)

Nobody's told them
subways are for sleeping:

a hundred eyes on them
but they only laugh
in their aloneness

at the loveless.

340

SKATER

This morning for the first time
I didn't laugh at her.
Perhaps because she had the rink
all to herself on this March day
of twenty-mile-an-hour wind blowing cold
across Nathan Phillips Square, all to herself
to practise her slow reverse turns
around a corner of the ice, oblivious it seemed
to the same wind that blew me,
rudderless iceboat, over that slippery stretch,
and making me see for the first time
what I'd been stubbornly blind to before:

this woman, forty-five, fifty, suddenly graceful
in her awkward stance, child-like wonderful
in the way arms turned, whole body completely
in love with the motion, almost dizzy with the joy
now seizing her limbs!

And all this on a bitter March morning,
with me late for work, but not caring now,
my feet on the ice, gliding, turning with her!

341

THE GIFT

To see his delight
to be given a newly cut
handful of flowers,

to watch how he holds them
tightly yet tenderly
as he walks across the Square.

Old wizened-up Chinaman,
you have made this morning for me,

from now on all flowers
will be carried this way!

342

PICTURES FROM A LONG-LOST WORLD: THE STACKER, WESTERN FRONT, 1917

Perhaps because he doesn't know he's being watched, this stacker of bodies goes about his business naturally, relaxed, not with the military stiffness he might adopt, say, if the Inspector-General were in the vicinity.

This morning he's being kept fairly busy, the stretcher-bearers bringing in one corpse after another, which they dump very casually on the ground, then go back to make another pickup. His job, then, is to lift these dead bodies up so they form neat, orderly piles on the large flat carts made especially for the purpose. He's well chosen for the job, being a tall, heavy man who seems to handle the bodies quite easily. As he picks one up he turns each body so that it rests face down on the pile. Sometimes he doesn't get one placed exactly right, the head perhaps sticking out several inches beyond the others; and, being the perfectionist he is, he'll tug or push that particular body to get it exactly back in line—once he even uses a kick when his hands don't seem to be making the right progress. He's also a sensitive man, even with day after day of this bloody work, and where a neck shows without a head he'll cover it over with a piece of burlap standing by for just such a purpose.

Then, when he can't lift any more bodies onto the first pile of a new cart, he completes the layer he's working on to his satisfaction and begins another fresh stack. It's hard work and he has to admit to himself that he's beginning to feel his age. He'll be glad indeed when the new helper the sergeant has promised him arrives. He hopes he'll be an older man like himself—young people nowadays don't seem to take any pride in a job well done. Why, if only the dead could see themselves lying here now he feels sure even they would be struck by the soldierly neatness of things, all ends properly in place, so to speak, everything done with precision and despatch as on the most exacting of parade-squares!

LAST CARRY

You were small but wiry,
and on the football field
hard to catch, hard to tackle;
I used to curse
every time they gave you the ball
for an end-run carry.

Twenty-seven years ago
right to this very day,
while you were still learning
a new game called War
in flooded, ravaged Holland,

a German 88
must have read the play,
was waiting when you made
your sweep around the end,
moved in, crashed you down
for your last carry ever.

344

BAY STREET

Fired this week
after forty years' service.

Yes, he's had an alcoholic problem
for a long, long time, but they waited
until this year to axe him,

year of 1970,
year of cutbacks,
of the tightening of the belt,
elimination of frills
and unnecessary expenditures.

345

THE SPIDER OUTSIDE OUR WINDOW

The spider outside our window
had a problem. A chunk of rose petal
in falling had grabbed hold
of his net and stayed there,
somehow content.

What to do? Charlie didn't like
the taste of it, the thing took up
far too much trapping area,
and yet gave the place a little class
sadly lacking before, so he dallied,
not moving it.

Then one day, inspiration!
He lettered up a sign in bug's blood,
hung it out proudly:

HAPPY CHARLIE'S ROSE GARDENS
WHERE YOU'LL ALWAYS MEET A FRIEND

THE PAPERS FROM HUNGARY

Their illustrated papers
arrive every week
in a language I don't understand.

On almost every page
the ever-smiling, contented faces
of ordinary people.

It's only when one escapes
or dies crossing the wire
at the frontier,

that we learn at last
that those faces can be sad
and even cry,

the same as yours or mine—
we, naïve victims
of the exploiters
in the dying West.

347

LAST DRUM-BEAT FOR ROSE LAROSE

(DIED. *Rose LaRose, 59, ecdysiast extraordinary whose artistry
as a burlesque stripper earned her $2000 a week during the
nineteen-forties; in Toledo.)*

The Casino must have stood about here,
"Toronto's only burlesque,"
featuring one week only
THE EXOTIC ROSE LAROSE:

which would place the stage about here,
the spotlight coming on at the left
to bathe in a rapid succession of reds, blues, greens, yellows,
the face of Rose LaRose now appearing,
the filmy-dressed form of Rose LaRose now gliding
across that stage as the five-piece pit band
begins the sultry, muted strains
of *Caravan*, Rose still gliding, side-stepping
once more around the stage before she removes
first her gloves slowly, then the veil, then the shoulder wrap,
handing them off each time she nears the curtain,
while the music builds as with a flick of wrists
she stands in tights flashing wild star-dust at us.

Moving now panther-like, lithe tigress,
paces the stage once, turns, fingers leisurely removing
the slight brassière, to stand squarely facing us,
breasts taunting us so hugely, slightly quivering,
only the nipples hidden now:

then slowly, surely, mask of her face expressionless,
starts in to shake them, left, right, left, right,
until the great shivering globes blur in one unending
feast of flesh abandoned now to madness, sheer madness!

348

Then stop to a drum-beat! Her hips suddenly quiet,
those breasts two unbelievables still—
though motionless, at rest—but only for a moment:
now she starts in to sway that generous body
as the drum-beats summon, moving to the footlights' edge,
breasts, thighs, crotch all writhing, gyrating now,
caught up in the rhythm's spell!

And here the big finale begins
with a one, two, three, four, five and six,
to the pit drum's crashing roll, the bump and grind,
Rose like a savage now throwing it, drawing back,
throwing it out at us once again,
saving one final twist as the spotlight fades
and the stage that would have been about here turns to
    darkness,
with the theatre seats once about here wrapped in sweat
to the last high row of the balcony,
and the pit band coming on strong
with its raucous blare telling us the show is ended
(O how we know that it's ended!)

And that sex-goddess face and form of Rose LaRose
hot in our minds as we stumble out on Queen Street,
the doors opening then about here on the warm, smoky,
    summer-night air,
where today two steam-shovels prod the frozen earth
onto monster dump trucks, thirty feet below
the dressing room where Rose LaRose once returning,
passed a towel across her firm, warm, wonderful backside,
then sat like a queen at her dressing-table,
smoking a well-earned cigarette.

Abandon of Cats, The, 68
Acorn, The, 76
Air-Force Chaplain, 44
Air-Raid Practice, 160
All Animals Like Me, 100
Almost Last Visit to an Old Town, 294
Ambulance, 18
Angels, The, 230
Another Day, 26
April Fourth, 77
Armadale Avenue Revisited, 87
At the Airport, 146
At the Polanyis', 164
At the Wedding Party, 214
At this Moment, 215
August Garden, 212
Back Lane, 335
Backwater, 228
Bad Luck, 93
Battered, 232
Bay Street, 345
Beautiful Children, 39
Bed from Holland, The, 199
Be the Weed-Cutter, 60
Beyond, 146
Big Al at the Kicking-Horse, 270
Big Freeze, The, 250
Bill, 184
Black Ant, 43
Blind Girl, 20
Bocce Players, September, 163
Boldt's Castle, 167
Boy Playing with Mud, 92
Bride, The, 85
Broken Bottle, 120
Broken Day, 112
Bud, The, 169
Burial, The, 19
Bus Stop, 161
Butterfly on Melinda Street, 170
Cage, The, 295
Calamity the Cat, 111
Calling on Leroi, 114

Can it Be?, 147
Cave, The, 32
Change, The, 34
Changes, The, 97
Chasing the Puck, 213
Chemnitz Attack, February 14/15, 1945, 308
Chimney, The, 229
Christ on Yonge Street, A, 195
Christmas Dinner, 106
Church Bells, Montreal, 82
Cicada, 51
Cicada Madness, 239
Clock in the Kitchen, The, 57
Close to Home, 296
Compensation, 159
Confidences of Spring, The, 116
Confrontation, The, 289
Crazy Spring Song, 148
Critic, The, 290
Cry, The, 171
Dandelion, 28
Day Before Christmas, The, 124
Death Chant for Mr. Johnson's America, 282
Death in Rutherford, A, 74
Death on the Construction Site, 275
Decision on King Street, 28
Demolition in August, 310
Dogs of Korea, The, 27
Don't Laugh, 278
Downtown Train, 217
Dresden Special, The, 244
Driftwood, 206
Drunk Down the Street, The, 109
Ducks, Five O'Clock, Late November, 248
Easter Sunday, 17
Eddie Condon at the New Colonial, 14
Embarrassment, The, 204
End of February, The, 233
End of Summer, The, 330
Evergreen in Winter, 84

Explanation, The, 247
Extra Blanket, The, 16
Eye, The, 261
Face of Cleveland, The, 49
Farm Out the Sydenham Road, The, 174
February Wind, 332
Fireworks, 95
First Holiday Morning, 331
First Report to the Military Governor, 302
First Scarlet Tanager, The, 196
First Snowflake, 297
First Two Acorns, The, 218
Fisherman, 22
Five Nighthawks, 292
Flotsam, 62
Foghorn, 67
Fool's Day, 300
For Bay Street Charlie, 320
Forecast, 307
For Ikuko from the Two of Us, 317
For John Pocock's Daughter, 201
For Padraig, 232
Fortress, The, 35
Four Girls at the Corner, 33
Freeze-Up, 42
Full Blossom, 246
Funeral Director, 188
Funeral Oration, 138
Garbage in the Morning, 234
General Brock at Fort George, 134
Get the Poem Outdoors, 224
Gift, The, 342
Girl in the Blue Bikini, 24
Girls of the Morning, The, 265
Go Ask, 54
Good Doctor, The, 137
Good Dog Sam, 221
Good Fortune, 50
Great Beast of the Fog, 84
Great White Locusts, The, 298
Grey Squirrel, Central Park, 23
Grigio, 280

Groundhog's My Nature, 21
Gwendolyn MacEwen at the Bohemian Embassy, 108
Hallelujah, 200
Hawk, 48
Her Highness, 90
Hippies at Nathan Phillips Square, The, 288
Holding Hands in the Library, 334
Homecoming, 22
House, The, 305
House on Indian Road, The, 154
How Natural is Gas, 186
How to Skip Stones on a Rough Day, 212
Hurdy-Gurdy in the Snow, 180
Ice Valley, 249
I Like to Imagine, 184
Immigrant, The, 173
In a Moment of Anger, 324
Interruption, The, 199
In the Barn, 58
Into Night, 128
It's Not That Easy, 306
Jazzman, 135
Jewels, 277
John Sutherland, 1919–56, 192
Journey, 127
Kensington Market, 129
Killing a Bat, 208
Kind of *Voyeur*, A, 299
King Street Station, 120
Kite, 130
La Crosse, 273
Last Batter, The, 253
Last Beer at the Towne, 13
Last Bonfire, 90
Last Carry, 344
Last Drum-Beat for Rose LaRose, 348
Last Ice on Bass Lake, 47
Last Piece of Bread, The, 186
Late Arrival, 226
Laura Secord, 94

Leaf Man, The, 133
Letter to Biafra, 281
Light, The, 102
Lilac Bush in Winter, 23
Little Boy Lost, 271
Long, Long Winter, 99
Looking at Old Photographs, 115
Loyalist Burial Ground, Saint John,
    21
Mackenzie's House, 78
Man Who Finds Love on the Subway,
    The, 24
Man with Clubfoot, 304
Maple, 149
Marriage Bit, The, 185
Maryrose Visits the Toronto Stock
    Exchange, 64
Max, 268
Mechanical Stump-Remover, 71
Meeting in the Subway, 269
Memory of Bathurst Street, 118
Metamorphosis, 91
Migration, 172
Milk-Chocolate Girl, 153
Mirror, The, 247
Montreal '65, 158
More Interruptions Like This, Please,
    276
More on Drunken Clocks, 12
Morning of Grey Rain, 117
Motives, The, 52
Mourning Dove, 301
Moving Day, 131
"Mr. Hill", 83
My Two Poplars, 107
National War Memorial, 237
Never Look Back, 185
News of the Day, 156
Night Over Huron, 132
Night Raider, 142
Night With Slow Freights, 187
1944, 148
Nineteenth-Century Music-Box, 107
Ninety Ducks, 15

Ninety in the Shade, 51
Nobody's Told the Birds, 157
Not Really for Publication, 305
Now That April's Here, 340
Now the Mulberry's Fruit, 272
Now We Take You to Biafra, 267
Observation Ward, 109
Ocean Limited Leaving Bonaventure
    Station, 1943, 58
October Moon, 29
Offering, 97
Old Cemetery, Queen's, 56
Old Farms, Bruce Peninsula, 113
Old Lake Light, Hanlan's Point, 318
Old Man Crossing the Farmyard, 59
Old Mill by Moonlight, 339
Old Veterans, Battery Dinner, 260
On Georgian Bay, 80
On Our First Day of May, 196
On the Island, 203
On the Road to Wiarton, 103
On the Rouge, 136
Ottawa for Me, 325
Pact, 236
Papers from Hungary, The, 347
Parade, The, 110
Peace Demonstration, 291
Pee Wee, 81
Pensioners in the Park, 201
Petition, The, 262
Picker of Dandelions, A, 162
Pictures from a Long-Lost World:
    1912, 329
Pictures from a Long-Lost World:
    The Stacker, Western Front, 1917,
    343
Pictures from a Long-Lost World:
    A Morning in Brussels, 1943, 73
Pink and Blue Balloons, The, 36
Pitching Apples, 231
Poem for Francine, 17
Pomegranates in Studio One, 225
Portrait of the Artist as a Young Man
    Well-Rolled in Montreal, 316

Prayer and a Sacrilege, The, 190
Praying Mantis, A, 274
Prelude, 20
Problem, The, 293
Problem of Skating, The, 25
Quarrel, The, 63
Queen Anne's Lace, 338
Rainbow Over Lake Simcoe, 43
Rain is Only the River, The, 30
Red Roses on the Trellis, 188
Remembrances, 293
Riding Out, 121
Rites, The, 145
Ritual, The, 62
Roses, The, 206
Roundhouse, The, 66
Say Goodbye, 191
Scream, The, 68
Send-Off, 230
Seven Days of Looking at a Rubber
    Plant, 139
Shadow, A, 198
Sharing, A, 207
Shipwrecked, 328
Shoe-Store, 241
Show Time, 209
Sign of the Times, 110
Sign, The, 330
Silence, 30
Simile, 35
Sirens, The, 182
Skater, 341
Small Coloured Stones, The, 209
Small House in a Small Town, 281
Snowplough, 326
Snows of Summer, The, 181
So Easy to Explain, 143
Some Canadians, 240
Some Small Green Buds, 82
Song, The, 219
Sparrow Supper, 104
Spider Outside Our Window, The,
    346
Spring Soaking, 183

Spring Waits for Me, 46
St. Catherine Street East, 75
Stone, The, 38
Stopping by the Side of the Road, 152
Summer Camp for the Blind, 111
Summer Falling, 264
Summer Shower, 119
Sunday Morning in the Park, 126
Swan, Midhurst Park, 19
Swansea Spring, 45
Ten Elephants on Yonge Street, 70
Tenement, 76
Thaw, 147
There's No Way Out of It, 258
They Said, 42
Thickson's, 151
Thirteen Days of Death, 336
This Last Dopey Fly, 92
This Lizard of Summer, 85
This Rose, 333
This Wind, 31
Three Sounds in the Valley, 55
Thrush, 45
Thursday Night Out, 235
To Have the Patience, 29
Tom Fisher's Mill, 99
Top Secret, 279
Touch, The, 327
Tracks in the Snow, 326
Tragedy, The, 36
Tryst, 96
Twelve Daffodils at Easter, 216
Twenty-Eight Million Market, 98
Twin Sittings, 150
Two Taunting Crows, 298
Unadulterated Poetry, 152
Unbelievable, The, 89
Underpass, The, 216
Very Short Poem, 246
Visit, The, 198
Waiting for Rain, 245
Waiting for the Rain to End, 303
Walk in the Park, A, 161
Walking October's Streets, 205

Walking River-Ice, 96
Walking through Sackville, 220
Wall, The, 149
Wasp Nest, 189
Waters, 202
Wedding Night, 105
Weeping Willow, 210
Weeping Willow, Early Spring, 187
Weeping Willow in Winter, 243
We were Innocents Then, 227
What the Camera Never Catches, 222
Whistler, The, 86
White Bedsheet, The, 144
Who Knows, 54
Wild Canary, 60
Wild One, The, 251

Wild Wolves of Winter, The, 37
Winter Break, 101
Winter Valley, 65
Witness from Jehovah, A, 205
Words for Kellie Jones Alone, 104
Words, The, 207
World of the Waterfall, 53
Worm, The, 183
Worm from the Centre of the World, The, 252
Wrapper, The, 38
Wreckers' Progress, 339
Wrecking-Ball, 72
Yeah, Tigers, 259
Yorkville Avenue, 324
You are the One Bird Singing, 89